D0167126

The Valuable Office Professional

The Valuable Office Professional

For Administrative Assistants, Office Managers, Secretaries, and Other Support Staff

Michelle Burke

amacom

American Management Association

New York · Atlanta · Boston · Chicago · Kansas City · San Francisco · Washington, D.C.
Brussels · Mexico City · Tokyo · Toronto

Library of Congress Cataloging-in-Publication Data

Burke, Michelle Marie.
    The valuable office professional : for administrative assistants,
office managers, secretaries, and other support staff / Michelle
Marie Burke.
       p.   cm.
    Includes index.
    ISBN 0-8144-7888-3
    1. Clerical occupations.   2. Managing your boss.   I. Title.
HF5547.5.B863   1996
651.3—dc20   96-9493
                                                      CIP

Printing number

To all administrative support staff for their valuable contributions and for the difference they make to the success of their organizations

In memory of
Lee Ann Pearson,
who inspired me with her creativity and showed me that it is possible to be both feminine and powerful

Table of Contents

Acknowledgments   *ix*

Letter to Support Staff   *xiii*

Introduction   1

Part One
The Principles of Changing Perceptions   **5**

1 The Changing Organization: From Support Staff
   to Office Professionals   7
2 Shifting the Administrative Paradigm   15
3 The Productivity Factor   25

Part Two
The Five Core Competencies   **45**

4 Basic Training: The Core Competencies   47
5 The Buck Stops Here: Accountability   60
6 You've Gotta Believe: Barriers Are Opportunities   74
7 Getting On Track: Commitment to Results   90
8 In With the New: Adopting a Desire to Learn   99
9 Bridging the Gap: Effective Communication   108

Part Three
The Productivity Cycle™   119

10 Putting It All Together: The Productivity Cycle™   121
11 Making Clear Requests: Phases I, II, and III   127
12 Making Purposeful Decisions and Achieving
    Goals: Phases IV and V   143
13 Completing and Implementing Decisions: Phases
    VI, VII, and VIII   156

Part Four
Conclusion   163

14 A Bridge Complete: Some Final Thoughts   165

    Index   *169*

Acknowledgments

This book was written through the collaboration of many minds. Five years ago when I started my own company, I also began contemplating this book. It has been a work in progress until now. I am forever grateful for the support, wisdom, and inspiration that I have received over the years from the many creative thinkers in my life. Their contributions made this book possible.

For the development and production of this book, I am deeply grateful, first and foremost, to my family. Their love, support, continued words of encouragement, and, best of all, their great sense of humor have given me the strength, persistence, and motivation to complete this book:

- To my parents—my father, Robert Burke, and my mother, Chris Kelly—who instilled in me a strong sense of self, a belief and a faith that anything is possible, and, most of all, their unconditional love.
- To my brother, Michael, for his positive words of encouragement, humor, and, with his wife, Karey, and his daughter, Riley, for demonstrating how great life can be.
- To my sister, Sue, who made me laugh when I needed it most, for her great suggestions, especially for Chapter 7, and for her constant support and friendship.
- To my grandmother, Madeline, for her love, prayers, and many words of wisdom.

I also wish to acknowledge my friends and associates in business who have offered their valuable insights, inspiration, and learning over the years:

- My mentor, friend, and colleague, Charles Amico, for his continued belief in me and my work and for giving me the opportunity of a lifetime—my first job as a consultant. Also, I am grateful for his willingness to share his expertise, insights, and wisdom to enrich my professional and personal growth.
- My literary agent, Sheryl B. Fullerton, for believing in this project and in me and for finding a publisher who did, too! And to my editor, Laurel Olson Cook, for her excellent suggestions, attention to detail, and commitment to this book.
- My friend, Kim O'Neill, for her dedication and endless hours of reading and editing and for her many great suggestions.
- Valerie Beeman of Stanford University and Kori Peterson of Intel Corporation for believing that administrative support staff are an integral part of the organization and for giving me the opportunity to train support staff.
- Susan Hoffer, Ph.D., for her expertise in making the assessment tool a valuable instrument.
- Jamie E. Barclay of Innovative Design Solutions for her great graphics. Without her creativity, standards of excellence, and long hours, this book would not have been possible.
- Jane Farley Tillman for her innovative graphic designs.
- Siobhan Collopy, who took time out of her busy schedule and offered her expert technical support and especially her commitment to excellence to make this book a success.
- Michael Collopy for his expertise and for his keen, creative photographic style and especially for making me look good.
- James Milojkovic, Ph.D., and John Thompson, Ph.D., who inspired me to continually move forward through their insights and knowledge, which greatly enriched my thinking.
- Andrea Iadanza and Sylvia Hayes of the American Management Association, Susan Fenner of Professional Secretaries International, and Ellen Bravo and Carmen Murguia of Nine to Five Organization for Working Women for ac-

knowledging the value of administrative support staff and their commitment to making a difference through their national and international conferences and other public efforts.

And finally, to my incredible, supportive, and inspiring friends—especially Bettina, Ellen, Jeanne, Joan, Jon, Judith, Katherine . . . and Paul for being there when I needed someone the most, for keeping me focused, and for teaching me patience— thank you all for the love and laughter that you have brought into my life. I am truly blessed.

Letter to Support Staff

This book was written in honor of you and the valuable contributions you make daily to your managers and organizations. I felt it was important to publicly acknowledge the efforts and hard work that you do. I, too, was once an executive assistant, and I know the difficulties, challenges, and rewards that come with that job. I spent more than ten years in the role, which supported me while I earned my college degree. I learned a lot from the various managers I supported over the years, and that learning, coupled with research and training done as part of my business, Executive Counterparts™, led to this book.

I believe that you are the glue of the organization and what I consider to be the New Middle Management. After all, you are the ones who have taken on the responsibilities once performed by middle managers. I also know this job is not easy, and it is not for everyone. This is a complex and challenging role that requires a multitude of skills, a positive attitude, and an acceptance of the constant changes that are a definite part of the job.

This book is about empowering administrative support staff to take risks with managers and coworkers that will forever change society's and the business community's beliefs about you, beliefs that have prevailed for more than forty years. I believe that if you are to make a real difference in the business world, you must first believe that it is possible to make a difference. Collectively, administrative support staff have tremendous power and need to learn how to use it appropriately. Many years ago, when I was working with a certain chairman of the board, I learned the power of language. In this book I will explain how you can use this powerful tool to be heard.

With all of the technological advances and other organizational changes business has experienced, you are in a position to learn new tools, knowledge, and skills—competencies that can advance you in your jobs—and more important, bring you the credibility and acknowledgment that are long overdue. It is time for you to rise above being what has been perceived as "just a secretary"—to what I refer to as "the results producer"—and to begin to see yourself as the competent valued employee that you are. After reading this book, those of you who are willing to practice the tools and take new actions will not only have a great impact upon your organizations but also experience better communication and ultimately, greater job satisfaction.

If you are interested in sharing your thoughts, ideas, or experiences with me, you may contact me through Executive Counterparts in San Francisco, California.

May this book, *The Valuable Office Professional*, inspire and motivate you to take the risks to improve your working relationships and the quality of your work life.

The
Valuable
Office
Professional

Introduction

Imagine what would happen if all administrative support staff walked off their jobs today. Where would that leave their managers and the others who rely on them to fulfill a role that no one else can? Better yet, imagine what it would be like if managers had to do the job of their assistant as well as their own. Let's face it—the ramifications would be disastrous, not just for management but also for the company's ability to function as a whole. The impact would also be devastating for the profitability of the organization.

Despite knowing this, many managers and support staff still have an outdated perspective on the role of the assistant. Even though managers may see their assistants as functional parts of the organization, they don't acknowledge the expanded and critical role they play. Despite the increasing importance of the manager-assistant relationship, few organizations put any emphasis on strengthening that link or on solving the problems that arise. As a result, the relationship can suffer from a lack of clear communication, active teamwork, and well-defined expectations and goals. Those problems affect not just employee morale but also the organization's bottom line.

According to Ellen Bravo, executive director of Nine to Five Organization for Working Women, two distinct trends are affecting support staff in the 1990s. The first trend is positive because it focuses on the value of support staff. Managers and the business community are coming to view their assistants as essential to the overall success of the company and make every effort to make them part of the team. The second trend is less favorable to management and the business world, because it reflects an attitude that Bravo refers to as foolhardy; managers view their support staff as nonessential and easily replaceable, which is short-term thinking and self-defeating.

Some organizations that focus on skills training and consider themselves "best practices" companies have begun offering catalogue-type courses for their assistants. Typically, however, they address only the functional skills and not the managerial, interpersonal, and team-building skills that assistants need to succeed in their expanded role.

What is most surprising is that the manager-assistant relationship is one of the oldest in the workplace, and yet it is rarely seen for what it is: a team with enormous influence on organizational productivity and customer satisfaction. If the manager-assistant team does not function well, at the CEO level or lower, the effect on the organization is devastating. Especially today, with businesses downsizing, reorganizing, and restructuring as never before and with an avalanche of technological advances, the responsibilities of administrative support staff have increased dramatically. In fact, according to a survey in 1994 by Professional Secretaries International (PSI), support staff has taken over more than 70 percent of the responsibilities that were once performed by management. This statistic alone points to the rapidly changing environment we are living in today. What is unfortunate is that the salaries for administrative support staff have barely increased since the survey appeared. According to PSI the average salary for support staff ranges between $24,000 and $34,000, depending on job title. What does this say about the value organizations place on their trusted "right arms"?

It's hard to believe that support staff aren't respected more, recognized more, and paid more for the complex role they perform. More than 4.2 million women, according to a 1994 Bureau of Labor Statistics report, work in this capacity, making this the largest category of working women in the United States. And, that number is expected to grow by more than 250,000 by the 2005. Because the vast majority (98.9 percent) of support staff are women, I will refer to this role as *she* or *her* throughout the book.

With these statistics, you would think that support staff would have a greater impact on management and their organizations. Although there are a few companies that are progressive in their views about their employees and that include support staff as part of their team development process, there are far more companies that don't. This information is not meant to scare assistants away from making changes that could benefit them. Quite the contrary, it is meant to motivate them to change in a way that brings them the acknowledgment and recognition that they deserve and that is long overdue.

In order for this to happen, however, assistants need to be more proactive and to take a stronger stand for themselves. Over the past few years, I've had the opportunity to interview, train, and coach hundreds of support staff. The most common characteristic they share is a lack of confidence, not about their ability to do their jobs but about their ability to have their work needs and wants met, whether that means asking their manager to schedule daily or weekly meetings with them, asking for a pay increase on the basis of their performance, asking to be filled in on the bigger picture, asking for acknowledgment, or asking for a clear career path. It is time for support staff to stand up and be counted; after all, they are key to the success of every organization.

The Valuable Office Professional is about helping administrative support staff take accountability for the quality of their work life, since we spend more time at work than we do anywhere else. This book also argues that managers and assistants must work together as partners, not as two individuals attempting to achieve separate goals. There are a multitude of tools, tips, and interactive exercises, including the Five Core Competencies and the Productivity Cycle™, to help assistants meet the challenge of working as partners with their managers, especially when the managers don't see or want to see their assistants as partners or counterparts. We focus on attaining new knowledge, empowering teamwork, and inspiring professionalism in the workplace in order to bridge the communication and workstyle* gaps that exist between support staff and those they work with. Assistants will learn the importance of becoming more "response-able" for their role and for their own job satisfaction.

---

*A work style is how a person approaches her work, the way in which she gets her work done.

Part One
The Principles of Changing Perceptions

Chapter 1

The Changing Organization: From Support Staff to Office Professionals

Your ultimate success as administrative support staff relies on your ability and willingness to take risks, such as:

- Learning when to say no
- Learning how to ask for what you want
- Learning to be direct
- Learning to value and stand up for yourself
- Learning to be accountable
- Learning to think beyond the immediate task

And, most of all:

- Learning to savor the satisfaction that comes from learning

This chapter sets the stage for you to review your role through a historical lens and to see how changing your perspective and behavior can lead to greater job satisfaction and increased productivity. We will look at business trends and how they impact your role in the organization as well as what you have to look forward to in the future.

For a company to be successful, it must recognize the value of its employees, particularly support staff who produce 80 percent of the work in organizations. Second, it needs to spend adequate dollars to train that staff. Without a reliable corps of highly trained people, a company cannot exist, and without support staff in particular, no company can operate at its full potential—an absolute necessity if it is to be competitive globally. Because the goal of a business is to create products and/or services in order to make profit, the users of those products and services—the customer—must be satisfied. Providing good customer* service** and satisfaction*** is the ultimate goal, and those organizations that are savvy enough to value and train their employees will achieve it. Figure 1-1 illustrates how the use of knowledge over time leads to profits.

Companies that recognize the importance of training will lead other organizations into the twenty-first century. Tom Peters, in his book *Thriving on Chaos,* suggests that most U.S. companies spend too little time and resources on training their most valuable asset—their employees. He compares American companies with businesses in Germany, Japan, and elsewhere that have training budgets that put ours to shame. Furthermore, my research over the years has shown that administrative support staff are usually last on the list for training. The majority of organizations spend most of their training dollars on programs for management, sales, and technical support, and whatever is left over in their budget is used for those remaining. It is despicable that, as we move into the twenty-first century, support staff are still struggling to get the training they need and deserve. According to a Professional Secretaries International (PSI) 1994 survey, the top three areas that secretaries and office professionals need training in are: computer software, team building, and communication skills to enhance their careers.

Customers: People inside and outside your company who rely on you to produce specific business results, which they, in turn, use to produce results for their customers.
**Service:* Ensuring that all actions taken will meet or exceed the needs of your customer in a timely manner.
***Satisfaction:* A specific result that the customer requests in which the standards or expectations are met and acknowledged by the customer.

Figure 1-1. A Business Perspective.

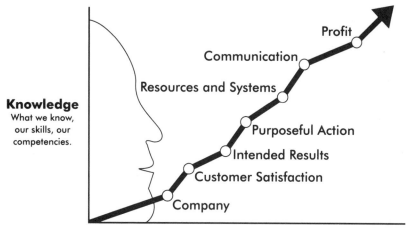

Knowledge
What we know,
our skills, our
competencies.

Profit

Communication

Resources and Systems

Purposeful Action

Intended Results

Customer Satisfaction

Company

Time
A company hires people with specific knowledge that will move the
organization forward for the purpose of creating a profit. This is done
by satisfying customers and by producing results through purposeful actions.
Having the proper resources and communicating
effectively over *time* will produce a profit.

The good news is that some progressive companies do recognize that support staff are an integral part of the organization and, more important, a real part of the team. Companies like Intel, Hewlett-Packard, Seagram Wine Classics, Northern Telecom, and Varian Associates are just a few of the companies that believe that it is necessary to train all employees if the companies are to be competitive and profitable. These companies not only get better qualified assistants; they keep them, largely because they are aware that it is more than typing, filing, and computer skills that make an assistant an asset to the company and that if they have satisfied employees, then they can count on them when the going gets tough.

It certainly helps to have a company that is pro-training, but what if you don't work for one of those organizations? Well, there is still hope. At least half of my clients were referred by assistants who saw a need in their departments or work teams and proactively went to their managers or human resources departments with a request for training. These assistants were able to explain the need for training and the benefits that the company would reap in return for the time off and the money spent. The evaluations I have received over the years speak to the positive impact training has on support staff and, equally important, on those they work with. This is one of the many ways support staff can and do make a difference for both themselves and their coworkers.

The Changing Office Scene

If you look back over the years, you'll see how far office support staff has come and how far it needs to go in areas besides training. In the historical progression from "girls" to "women," women have moved from manual typewriters that routinely broke their fingernails to dedicated word processors to full-fledged computers. Women have gone from doing long division on paper to using desktop and hand-held adding machines to using computer-embedded calculators. Many of you probably remember the days of carbon paper and the joy of simple copying machines, days before you mastered elaborate $10,000 machines that leave managers calling for their assistants to unclog jammed paper.

In recent years, the job categories *typist, stenographer,* and *secretary* have largely been absorbed by new job titles, such as *administrative executive assistant, project coordinator, client liaison,* and *office supervisor.* People in these titles are now being referred to as support staff. In fact, PSI recently voted during its July 1995 international conference in Seattle to add to its organizational name the tag line "the association for office professionals" because it wanted to acknowledge and include more than the title *secretary* in its membership of more than 40,000 office workers. This is another step forward for administrative support staff. The American Management Association has also recognized the need for this group (98 percent) of working women to be taken more seriously than in the past. AMA now sponsors a yearly national conference specifically for administrative assistants and executive secretaries.

Because of changing times, support staff are being given

more opportunities to expand their role and increase their knowledge base and skill sets. In the past ten years, administrators have had the opportunity to learn a wide variety of software and database programs designed by a multimillion-dollar industry where the demand for "new and improved" keeps eager programmers working into the wee hours so that it sometimes seems as if you no sooner learn to run a program than its update or successor is on the market. In this "information age," changes that directly affect your work lives occur faster than you can fax a memo across the globe.

You need only look at today's business trends to see what lies ahead. The business environment of the 1990s requires employees to challenge themselves, as individuals and as teams, to meet more of their clients' needs and to do so faster and better than before. Similarly, business needs higher-quality goods and services, shortened production cycles, and increased all-round productivity. Above all, in a tight economy with heightened competition for customers, customer satisfaction is more critical than ever.

Those who follow business trends have heard a lot about today's rapidly changing economy. They know that the rapid acceleration in computer technology has caused the world's markets to "shrink," creating what is frequently referred to as the global village. They know that instant communication now exists around the world and that differences in language and currency are no longer the barriers they once were. Along with these developments, managers at all levels have grabbed hold of the buzzwords *results-oriented, reengineering, diversity,* and *self-managing teams* as key components in this new business climate and have attempted to put them into practice. As companies downsize, the mere fact of trying to do more with less is taxing everyone and must ultimately affect the very productivity the company sought to improve in its decision to eliminate jobs and streamline operations. That is not to say that there is no "fat" to trim or that personnel needs and operations should not be reviewed for efficiency. But major restructuring demands careful monitoring, managerial sensitivity to and support for its workers, and—too often ignored— a company-sponsored education and training program for those remaining. Such programs are seldom made available to administrative support staff, and even fewer have been developed to explore the important question of how the working relationship between manager and assistant might need to be restructured if the company's "bottom-line" goals are to be achieved.

Given all of this, what is the place of the steadfast army of workers broadly referred to as support staff—the secretaries, the office supervisors, the executive assistants, the administrative assistants—who continue to hold together the paper kingdom of their managers and see to it that the myriad transactions and communications—the documents, reports, correspondence, invoices, and manuals—keep moving as they should? With fewer middle managers and more support staff, the breadth and range of responsibilities traditionally handled by the "secretary" is mushrooming. Although the administrative support role has often been mistakenly perceived as an "anyone-can-do-it" job, that is not the case. The job involves tremendous attention to detail, multitasking, flexibility, and a high level of professionalism and trustworthiness, not to mention possession of the functional and computer skills necessary to perform the job. Without a full-to-overflowing complement of technical, interpersonal, and team-building skills, administrative support staff cannot expect to compete successfully or advance in today's business market, whether she works for a lone entrepreneur in a home-based business or as part of a team of workers in a major corporation.

Even though the task may seem overwhelming, support staff are now in a position to move in directions that was never possible before. It begins with how you choose to view your role and the impact that has on your manager, team, department, and organization. This is the time to be seen as a "proactive counterpart" who believes that it is possible to excel in these times of change.

A major premise of this book is that, whether clerk or top executive assistant, you must hold yourself and the work you do in the highest esteem, to regard yourself as key contributor to your company, to think beyond tasks to larger company goals, and to be the catalyst in breaking down traditional power relationships between secretary and boss and replacing them with working partnerships. Achieving this takes more than repeating affirmations, useful as they are. It takes conscious effort, training, and practice of newly learned skills. Only when you shift your own perception of your role in the totality of the company and begin to act in accordance with that perception can you start to enroll others in dealing with you as a real part of the team.

From a human resources standpoint, the ultimate goal for a productive business in the 1990s and beyond is to develop relationships in which secretary and manager form a working partnership, each one contributing her separate skills to clearly articulated and mutually understood goals for the organization. The transformation required to move from outdated power relationships to working partnerships between managers and assistants involves four key elements:

1. An awareness of what was in the past
2. A clear vision of what can be in the present and future
3. A mutual agreement on clear expectations and goals
4. An action plan to put new practices into motion

By acting on these four elements, you can begin to achieve the kind of satisfaction that comes from understanding and realizing the tremendous contribution you make to your manager and to your organization. This naturally happens when you take purposeful actions that increase your productivity. To understand this concept further, let's define productivity. It is the power and the willingness to consistently produce quality results that are directly aligned with your managers' and companies' goals. Whether at the corporate or the individual level, being productive is more than just churning out work day after day like a robot. Being productive is about working smarter, not harder; doing the job better, not just differently; looking for ways to innovate and improve, not just changing for the sake of change. It is not about trying to do as many things as possible or completing as many tasks as you can. From the company's perspective, there is a significant cost savings and other benefits from an increase in productivity that they are willing to reward. Increased productivity can often mean an increase in pay or other benefits to acknowledge work well done. Furthermore, if you function more productively on the job, then you will ultimately find more time for home life and outside interests. Consequently, you will experience less stress, fewer illnesses, higher self-esteem, and more confidence. In short, life will become healthier and more balanced.

In this book, the focus is on how those in administrative support staff positions can, step by step, develop the tool box of skills required not just to hold down a job or keep the boss happy but to achieve real satisfaction. This comes from taking risks, changing your perspective about your role and being willing to take different actions. Change is never easy, and if you accept it as a constant rather than see it as an interruption, then you will have choices: You can fight it, go with it, or, better, anticipate it and take action.

I remember coaching one assistant, Sara, who was struggling with all of the changes going on in her organization, which was one of the many going through restructuring. She was given a whole new set of responsibilities because her manager was moving into a different position. Sara couldn't see that this was an opportunity for her to learn new skills, gain new knowledge about a different aspect of the company, and earn greater recognition for her work. Instead, she was struck in the way the company used to be and how it used to do things, and she did not hide the fact that she preferred it the old way. There are many Saras out there (who are what I call "change resisters"); they would prefer to keep things the way they are. Unfortunately, if you want to succeed in this rapidly changing environment, it's time to step up to the challenge of being a "change accepter."

In the rest of this book, I lay out the steps necessary for you to become a proactive executive counterpart, one who not only does the job right but does the right job better. They cover a broad range of skills and competencies, some having to do with attitude and style, others offering useful tips and techniques. Besides providing insights and information, this book includes a number of specific exercises drawn from the training programs I have developed. They reflect the situations, problems, and solutions I have encountered in my travels across the country and the feedback I have received from hundreds and hundreds of administrative support staff.

Chapter 2
Shifting the Administrative Paradigm

Much has been written about paradigms, particularly about the concept of "paradigm shift." Although usually discussed only by social scientists and social historians, the concept has a direct application to the theme of this book. What I am referring to is not just a shift in the relationship between assistants and their managers, but more importantly, a shift in our way of thinking about that relationship. And that is at the heart of the term, *shifting paradigms.*

So then what is a paradigm? A paradigm is the structure of how we perceive the world. It is based on past experiences, knowledge, and beliefs. From that perception, we take certain actions. A paradigm is thus how we "see" the world, not in the literal sense but how we understand or interpret it.

Although the concept of paradigms has been around for many decades, not until the 1980s, when Joel Barker wrote the book *Discovering the Future,* did the concept of paradigms really affect the business world. Barker believed that the concept of paradigms and how they shift, or change, was critical to business success. This chapter explores the concept of paradigms and how they affect your role as an assistant. Before you can really understand the tools and concepts of this book, you need to understand how your own paradigms can stop you from getting what you want and need at work and, more important, how to make a paradigm shift.

The Paradigm Shift

For the purpose of this book, the best way to understand paradigms, related specifically to the role of the assistant, is to look at Figure 2-1.

The left side of the figure represents the "proactive counterpart," and the right side represents the "traditional assistant." Each side is a paradigm. If you perceive yourself to be a traditional assistant, then all of the actions you take, the attitudes you have, and the assumptions you make will be based on the beliefs you have about what the role of the assistant should be. This perception came from the different influences in your life—parents, teachers, church, friends, community, work environment, and society.

Figure 2-1. Shift in the Administrative Paradigm.

PROACTIVE COUNTERPART	TRADITIONAL ASSISTANT
• Owns job.	• "Rents" job.
• Focuses on results.	• Focuses on tasks.
• Takes initiative.	• Waits for direction.
• Innovates.	• Is driven by policies and procedures.
• Self-manages.	
• Is solution-minded.	• Is managed.
• Adapts to change.	• Is plagued by problems.
• Continually improves self and work.	• Resists change.
• Recognizes job's relevance.	• Prefers comfort and security of status quo.
• Consistently anticipates needs and meets them.	• Knows job objectives and responsibilities.
	• Follows "to do" list.

You will continue to operate as a traditional assistant until you see a need to change your perception about the role or are influenced to change either by circumstances or by other people. When you see that your beliefs or perceptions no longer make sense or are useful, you will change them. This is a "paradigm shift." The moment your perception or belief changes, a paradigm shift has occurred. It's as if a light has been turned on in your mind; you will suddenly have a different perception from what you saw before. Having been a traditional assistant, you will suddenly realize that you don't have to wait for your manger to tell you what to do, that you can take the initiative. This paradigm shift will dramatically change the way you do your work and how you interact with your manager and coworkers. In the case of the proactive counterpart, you may consider yourself an initiator in some areas but not in others; although you have an innovative attitude, you will still have your own paradigms about how work should be done. This creates your work style, which we will address in Chapter 3. The point is that whether you are a traditional assistant or a proactive counterpart, you will have paradigms, and it is your responsibility to become aware of those paradigms that keep you from moving toward your professional and personal goals.

Let's make the concept of paradigms even more clear. Imagine receiving a deck of playing cards with spades colored red instead of black. Would you naturally assume the red spades are black, as they are in a standards deck of cards? In 1949 Thomas Kuhn gave such cards to a test group, which did not notice the difference. When they were questioned, the group members clung to their belief that the spades they saw were black. This experiment demonstrated convincingly how far most people's behavior is filtered through the dominant belief systems, even to the point of denying obvious truths. Kuhn concluded that behavior is filtered through beliefs, so much so that we create reasons to justify what we see. On the basis of these studies and others, in 1962 Thomas Kuhn wrote what is now regarded as the classic work on paradigms, *The Structure of Scientific Revolutions*.

Since Barker's book, management has been familiar with the paradigm shift concept and has been trying to shift organizational paradigms, in many companies leading to what appears to some to be chaos. This is not a concern, according to Tom Peters, author of *Thriving on Chaos;* he suggests that chaos is necessary and that businesses need to adopt a "fix it even if it doesn't 'appear' broken attitude." This is the essence of how you can create a paradigm shift in your organization. You don't have to wait until something no longer works. You can be proactive and look for ways to do things differently. As a proactive assistant, you can look for ways to improve your job and your role as an assistant. The alternative attitude is to wait and see what happens (like the traditional assistant); then, in the chaos of organization change, you will be forced to shift paradigms or perhaps lose your job. When a paradigm shift occurs, then a whole new set of possibilities appears.

Changing the Office Paradigm

In an office, a paradigm shift will deal more with the relationship between managers and their support staffs than with the establishment of new policies and procedures. There is bound to be some chaos as some support staff members deny the change and continue to behave as they did in the past. Others who are willing to forge ahead into uncharted territories and break the rules of the game are definitely taking a risk worth taking. Sometimes you may find that the resistance comes from yourself. Wherever it lies, the fact is that when you try out that new idea, change an old policy or procedure, or shift the way you choose to relate to your coworkers and managers, you are often unknowingly trampling on an old set of rules, expectations, and long-held assumptions about "the way it's always been." Not conforming to company expectations, offending the company "culture," can get you tagged as "insubordinate" or as someone who has an "attitude" or even as someone who is not a team player. People often collude with those evaluations through their own negative talk ("What do I know? I only work here," "They don't pay me enough," "I guess I stepped out of line that time," "If I do or say that, I will lose my job"). After a few rebuffs, you may conclude that it's best to leave well enough alone.

If you do stop trying, however, how are assistants going to continue to achieve the respect and recognition they deserve? It takes each assistant making a change within her working relationship, and specifically with her manager. In the old paradigm managers took it for granted that their secretaries would make and bring them coffee every morning. Then, one day, some secretaries finally got the courage to say that they were not willing to do that anymore. This is when the shift occurred. Maybe you are thinking that they probably got fired; maybe some did, but some didn't. Each of us has an opportunity to shift a paradigm within our working relationship if we choose. Just think about the future and the possibilities that are available to you. What if you and your manager were operating in a real partnership, both contributing to the goals of the company, acknowledging your different skills and standing shoulder to shoulder to produce the result? Does this sound too good to be true? Look at the paradigm chart in Figure 2-2 to remind yourself where assistants were twenty and forty years ago, until individual women like yourself took a step and then another step and another and so on. Look at Figure 2-2 to see how things have progressed in the work arena and what the future might bring for those willing to forge new roles and create new productive partnerships with their managers.

According to Joel Barker, when a paradigm does shift, everyone involved goes back to "start"—that is, everyone affected by the shift is suddenly on equal footing. What meant success in the past, under the old paradigms, no longer guarantees success. With all of the restructuring and technological advances occurring in the 1990s, paradigms are constantly shifting. But "don't rock the boat" has never been the watchword of anyone who has achieved success in life, and it is certainly not the premise of this book. The good news is that we are already standing on the shoulders of many who have gone before. Tremendous strides have been made, for example, since the 1950s, when women were either typists, secretaries, nurses, or stewardesses, always playing a second fiddle. Much of what you will learn from this book is about not only doing the job differently but about doing a different job better.

With the passage of time and the changes in the way society

(*text continues on page 22*)

Figure 2-2. Administrative Paradigm Shifts Spanning Forty-Plus Years.

	1950s	1970s	1990s	Future
Attitudes and Perceptions	Job Title: Secretary	Broadened job titles	Variety of titles	Obsolete titles
	Wears dress or skirt	Pantsuits allowed	Choice of clothing	Many choices
	Low salary	Low salary/benefits	Negotiates salary/benefits	Pay increase
	Secretary not valued	Secretary undervalued	Assistant's work valued	Assistant valued
	Manager has the power	Power relationships	Team has the power	Partnerships
	Single/no children	Married/single mothers	Flexible hiring	Diverse workforce
	Has no career vision	Lateral career path	Upwardly mobile	Your choice
Skills and Responsibility	No decision making/no autonomy	Responsibility/without autonomy	Responsibility/with autonomy	Accountability
	Shorthand/dictaphone skills required	Shorthand/dictaphone skills expected	Optional skills	As-needed basis
	Task-oriented	Task-oriented	Task and results-oriented	Results-producer
	Work managed by boss	Takes initiative	Self-managing	Managing projects/resources/people
				Problem solver
	Filing, typing, phones	Word processing	Computer literate	Flexible location & hours
	9–5 day	Increased hours	Flexible and more hours	Advanced training
	Secretarial school	HS diploma/business school	Technical training/some college	

	Little or no training	Functional skills training*	Computer & assertiveness training	Teambuilding/communication skills
Technology	Manual typewriter	Electronic typewriter	Computers/software	Multi-interactive system
	Mimeograph machines	Basic copy machines	Multitask equipment	Paperless office
	Postal/delivery services	Telex technology	Fax machines	Various on-line services
	Rotary telephone/switchboard	Digital phone systems and answering machines	Voice-mail, teleconferencing, video conferencing	Computer-based/voice-activated systems
Behaviors	Never queries manager	Queries manager if needed	Queries manager as needed	Same as 90s
	Makes/serves coffee	Refuses coffee role	Will if . . .	Nonissue
	Takes harassment	Does not take harassment, but typically doesn't take legal action	Willing/able to sue	Continues to sue
	Follows orders	Asks questions after the fact	Asks questions to anticipate and plan	Anticipates
	Reactive	Responsive	Proactive	Anticipative

*Functional skills are the basic skills that one must have in order to be hired (i.e., typing, filing, answering phones, coordinating travel).

looks at women, office assistants have made some important gains since the 1950s. Anyone can think of areas where change seems to be very slow and where it sometimes seems that women are not having the kind of impact they want and deserve; women can and need to shift those paradigms that keeping them from having what they want and deserve.

Returning to the chart, for example, the shape of things to come—the items listed in the "Future" column—won't take place unless you are willing to take some risks. Moving ahead, breaking new ground, is always a bit scary. *Feel the fear and do it anyway.*

In the traditional role of the secretary, your responsibilities were to do the following:

- Perform individual tasks assigned by your manager.
- Implement set policies according to set procedures.
- Organize all paperwork that passed over your desk.
- Focus on daily "to-do" lists.
- Anticipate and satisfy your boss's work needs.
- Know your place.

These were not functions anyone particularly railed against; the secretaries of the day just keep swimming around in that tank. The parental and societal message was strong: Find a job that offers a stable, highly structured work environment where job responsibilities are well defined, the hours are a steady, predictable 9-to-5, and you can count on a secure future. Even if she had wanted to, the secretary of the day was certainly discouraged from knowing anything about the company's "big picture" plans. The secretary with the best chance of being hired and staying with the company was generally detail-oriented, unassertive, and without ambition—except to get an annual percentage increase in salary, with perhaps the bonus of finding a husband.

In the aftermath of the 1960s there was a significant paradigm shift in American society, on the personal, professional, and institutional levels. Attitudes about nearly everything underwent major change; certainly the stereotypical roles assigned to women and the whole notion of "power relationship" and "authority" would never be the same again.

The 1960s and 1970s were tumultuous times for many but especially for women as they fought for seemingly small gains:

- The right to wear pantsuits to the office
- The right to expect others, including the boss, to pour their own coffee
- The right to be called "Ms.," not "Miss" or "Mrs."; "women," not "girls" or "ladies"; and to be referred to by last names as well as first, at least until familiarity was appropriate

It took much time to convince people, including many women, that these seemingly small things had effectively kept women demeaned, belittled, and disempowered. Women who were (and remain) unable to see the impact and the social significance of these social practices were very much like the card players who were unable to see the spades on the playing cards as red and not black. While these individuals were locked into another paradigm and simply didn't realize it, others, then and now, realized that changing these deeply entrenched behaviors was very likely to throw their personal and professional world into chaos.

The world has changed considerably, for men as well as for women. In the workplace, the boom days of the 1980s are over. At the midpoint of the nineties, we are experiencing an unrelenting economic upheaval that has resulted in widespread downsizing of large corporations. The very word "downsizing" was invented to describe what was going on all over the country—massive layoffs—as businesses once regarded as rock-solid (i.e., IBM) found themselves in financial distress.

Both downsizing and another common symptom of changing times—restructuring—have direct and immediate effects on office workers and on relationships among coworkers and managers. Those whose skills, whose company "fit," whose attitude, whose productivity is in question will find themselves reading the want ads. Employees who remain will be expected to take on more, do it faster and better, and probably answer to more than one manager. A look at the help wanted section of any major newspaper is enough to reveal the sharply increased demands being placed on the role of assistant, who now needs to have a "take-charge" personality, be a team player, know more than one computer system, be skilled in accounting software . . . the list goes on. From the company perspective, maintaining high-quality products or services, giving consumers good value for their dollars, and ensuring customer satisfaction in these lean times means letting go of old hierarchies and top-down leadership. If you can come up with a better system, you must be heard. If you are willing to go an extra mile for the company in these tough times, you must be listened to and respected. If you are to do your best for the company, the company must agree to let you in on the "big picture" planning process. Moreover, it is you who must educate management—specifically, your own boss—about the importance to the company of your taking on these new roles. If you are not willing to take these risks, open up these conversations with your managers, try out new procedures, some "proactive counterpart" waiting in the wings will certainly do so. So let it be you! This is the first step in shifting any paradigm.

Reminder: Be aware of those red spades. They can, and will, show up anywhere!

Chapter 3
The Productivity Factor

Terry walks into her assistant's office for the fifth time that morning. "Chris, where is the latest financial report? I need the new figures to fax to Judy Gonzalez for our conference call at 2:30 this afternoon. Make seven copies for everyone on the call. Oh, and book my trip to New York. I'm leaving Friday afternoon. I also need the 1996 fiscal year reports to take with me." Chris adds six more tasks to her already long "to do" list as she frantically tries to recall where she last saw that financial report. Terry yells from her office: "Where are Mr. Mark Chin and I having lunch today?" Chris doesn't answer because she forgot to make the reservation. She calls the Four Seasons and luckily gets a 1:00 P.M. reservation, and reports back to Terry. At 2:25 she rushes the report to Terry for her 2:30 call and informs her that the copier has broken down so she'll have to print the other copies from her computer. Terry scans the report and realizes that pertinent information is missing. Chris says, "I'm not sure it's not in the report. I'll print out another copy." She hurries to her computer frustrated and upset with Terry and herself.

Sound familiar? It is obvious that Chris and Terry are not working together as a team, and because of this they are not maximizing their productivity. Terry is making many demands on Chris and delegates tasks one at a time. Chris is overwhelmed by everything she has to do and is making mistakes. Given their dynamics, what is the greatest challenge they face as they team to work together better? The real problem is that Terry and Chris don't know how to deal with each other's different work styles, nor do they know how to work together as a team. As we discover more about work styles and learn more about what it means to be and act like a team, Terry and Chris will improve their productivity and job satisfaction.

The Link Between Productivity and Work Styles

This chapter focuses on the importance of knowing your work style and how it affects your productivity. Using the Productivity Checklists, you will have the opportunity to assess your work style and see how it affects your ability to work effectively with your manager.

Many work relationships become more productive when the people in them each become aware of their own strengths and abilities. No one can be productive until she has taken an inventory of what skills she possesses and what she brings to the team. This is especially true today, given the competitive business environment that prevails. Companies, large and small, are striving more than ever to produce the goods and services that will meet the specific, changing needs of their customers. They cannot do so without employees who are willing to give consistently high performance aimed at producing the results each company needs to meet its objectives and goals.

Whether at the corporate or the individual level, being "productive" is more than just churning out the work day after day like robots. As mentioned in Chapter 1, productivity in the 1990s is the ability and the willingness to consistently create quality results that are in alignment with the goals of the organization. The best way to do this is with the help of managers and teams. Once you know your work style, you can learn to function more productively using the actions suggested by the work style profiles in this chapter. If you do, you will experience one or more of the following positive outcomes:

- Increased job satisfaction
- Improved working relationships (particularly with your manager)
- Increased self-esteem and morale
- Greater self-respect and respect from coworkers

- Less overtime
- Less sick time
- Lower stress level
- Less time wasted on "what to do next"
- More or better career opportunities
- More possibilities for promotion and pay increase

If you consider that more than 60 percent of health care costs are due to unhealthy lifestyle habits, you'll see clearly that when you decide to adjust your work style and feel the benefits of that change in all areas of your life, your company will incur significantly lower health care costs and will most likely gain revenue from those changes.

It is therefore in the company's best interest for assistants to have all the tools that will help them become more productive. The first step in improving productivity is to take a look at the work styles that characterize the ways assistants approach their work. Knowing your work style and assessing its compatibility with that of your manager is key if you are to work as a team.

Everyone, no matter what her job, develops a work style over time, a way of approaching and managing her work. This approach to work is firmly established in a number of personal factors, including personality, experience, specific skills and competencies, need for social contact, and attitudes about being managed and managing. In addition to the personal preferences and characteristics people bring to the table external factors, such as office politics, organization culture, work environment (space aesthetics), and benefits, influence the specific demands of their jobs, the degree of choice they exercised when accepting their position and/or promotion, and whether they are good matches for their organization's "culture."

You may consider yourself "people-oriented" or a "lone wolf" when it comes to your general work preference, but if you are to achieve optimal satisfaction and productivity in your job, a more detailed assessment is necessary. Self-assessment and feedback, assuming they are approached in the right spirit, can be revitalizing at any time, but they are critical in the following circumstances:

- Your manager has been replaced.
- Your workload and/or responsibilities have changed.
- Your current working relationship(s) are unsatisfactory—they are not working.
- Your company is changing—restructuring, downsizing, etc.

To facilitate taking a hard look at who you are in the workplace, try completing the worksheet in the next section. The relationships you have with your manager and your coworkers, of course, involve two or more people; for the moment, however, focus on yourself. Look at yourself from your manager's perspective as much as from your own. Be honest in completing these exercises. Remember, knowing yourself is a key first step to all the relationships you will form in life. The intent here is not to blame or ridicule or make you defensive. Far from it. The purpose of these exercises is to open your eyes to who you are now and who you can be, to trigger insights about what might help you be more satisfied, productive, and challenged at your job. For some, the results may clue you in to what it will take for you to become indispensable to your company, if that is something you want.

Work Style Profiles

Through my work in this field, I have found that the following "clusters" of traits typify the major work styles found among support staff. Naturally, there will be some overlap from one style to another but, in general, the category where you find yourself making the most check marks will be your dominant style. I want you to know that these profiles are meant to inform, not to label or imprison you. Before you can change your behavior, you need to confront them. Only then can you learn what you can change and what you want to change about your approach to your job. Armed with that information, you will have a better basis for assessing what others—your manager and your coworkers—can contribute to create more productive team relationships.

Worksheet 1:
WORK STYLE PROFILES

When reading the items below for each work style profile, check off all statements that best describe your approach to work. At the end of each work style profile, total the number of check marks and enter that number on the "Total" line.

Work Style 1

_____ I am able to identify problems, but I look to my manager for solutions.
_____ I hesitate to make decisions without my manager's approval.
_____ I prefer to stick to routines and established procedures.
_____ I seldom offer ideas to improve my job.
_____ I think about long-range results only when asked to.
_____ I strictly follow my "to do" list.
_____ I avoid extra work or overtime when possible.
_____ I hesitate to accept assignments not in my job description.
_____ I strictly follow company policy and procedures.
_____ I let the "head honchos" worry about company goals.
_____ I see my manager(s) as an authority figure, not as a partner.
_____ I consider my job a necessity to "pay the rent."
_____ I frequently gripe to coworkers about my job and my manager.
_____ I focus on the tasks I need to complete, not on the result.
_____ I meet with my manager only when I absolutely have to.

Total ☐

Work Style 2

_____ I complete many tasks in a short period of time.
_____ I don't always make sure the work I am doing leads to my intended results.
_____ I work hard and fast every day.
_____ I tend to panic when I have too much work to do.
_____ I seldom ask for help, even when I know I need it.

_____ I am too busy to recognize or anticipate emerging problems or needs.
_____ I often feel overwhelmed by my many things to do.
_____ I often arrive early, work through lunch, or stay late to get caught up.
_____ I tend to work more than others.
_____ I resent the lack of balance in my life.
_____ I frequently feel unappreciated or unacknowledged for the work I do.
_____ I tend to focus on the immediate, short-term tasks.
_____ I operate in crisis mode much of the time.
_____ I seldom sit back to assess my work or prioritize tasks.
_____ I find it difficult to say no.

Total ☐

Work Style 3

_____ I take only purposeful actions.
_____ I meet my deadlines consistently.
_____ I understand the needs of my company's customers or clients.
_____ I consistently satisfy company goals and objectives.
_____ I anticipate and resolve problems early.
_____ I see work as an ongoing opportunity for skill building and personal self-improvement.
_____ I initiate regular consultations with my manager(s).
_____ I accept responsibility as a team member.
_____ I actively build and maintain trusting, results-oriented relationships with my manager and coworkers.
_____ I contribute to fulfilling the company's mission.
_____ I regard my work as much more than just a job.
_____ I feel satisfied at the end of the day and at the end of the week.
_____ I acknowledge others and myself for work well done.
_____ I create time for family, friends, and outside interests.

Total ☐

The category with the highest number of checks represents your primary working style at this particular time.

Read the following descriptions of the three work styles. These descriptions offer a brief summary of the work styles before we match them with a manager counterpart to see how people can work together better.

Now let's elaborate a bit by putting playful labels on each one.

Work Style 1—The Desk Potato

As a Desk Potato, you probably see your job as essentially a way to pay the rent. Although you get work done, you receive little personal satisfaction or challenge from the job. You tend to see your manager as "the boss," an authority figure with all the decision-making power and control. You rarely volunteer an idea or look for opportunities to improve the work routines, procedures, and systems or ask for additional responsibility, convinced no one will listen or that it's not your place to do so. You get some relief and enjoyment from confiding in coworkers and participating in gripe sessions during breaks or lunch time. You haven't though much about your career path or even if this kind of work is really for you.

Work Style 2—The Busy Bee

As a Busy Bee, you derive great satisfaction from consistently adding to, updating, and reprioritizing your "to do" list. You are constantly busy and sometimes wonder why others don't seem to have as much to do. When asked to do something, you always say yes, taking pride in your ability to handle whatever comes your way. You seldom ask for help, afraid you might appear incompetent. You tend to come in early or work late in order to stay on top of things, a habit that seems to annoy some coworkers. You like that you are perceived as "a hard worker" but sometimes feel undervalued. In addition, you can't seem to find enough time for your family or for your recreational needs.

Work Style 3—The Results Producer

You are someone who knows your value to your manager and to your company, and you routinely make important contributions to both. You see your relationships at work, whether with coworkers and teammates or with manager(s), board members, and VPs, as partnerships. You know the importance of building and maintaining trusting relationships with others, and you view your workplace as an arena that offers multiple opportunities for personal and professional growth. You are capable of setting clear priorities so that you can spend your time productively. You view your "to do" list as a tool for producing results, constantly reassessing the tasks to make sure they are relevant. You routinely meet deadlines and do not accept work requests you know you cannot complete. You enjoy anticipating needs and are comfortable offering ideas, solutions, and recommendations without being asked. You appreciate quality and strive to produce the best work in everything you do. You are mindful of the company's mission and of your manager's short- and long-range goals as they affect your role and those of your teammates. You like what you do and typically leave each day with a sense of satisfaction.

*   *   *   *   *

When evaluating how the various team combinations work together, you need to know the purpose of identifying your profile and that of your manager. Principally, this bit of knowledge serves as the basis for a conversation in which you discuss how each of you views team relationships in general and yours in particular, what works and what doesn't, and what needs to be improved. Remember, it is not for either side to point a finger of blame or to dispense with the other by labeling and consigning her to a box. That's a good way to create friction, not dispel it. Used well, these work styles and hypothetical scenarios are a simple tool that will guide you to productive team relationships.

Working Styles in Teams of Two

Now let's take a look at how the work styles we have identified come into play on the job. Some work relationships between assistants and managers just magically fall into place as you find yourselves serendipitously in tune with each other. Like romantic and marital relationships, work relationships take continual and conscientious care and effort.

When thinking about your work style profile, look also for the work style that best fits your manager. We have devised three different work styles that describe some typical managers. What if we put together the Desk Potato with what we'll call the "Clueless Manager"? Or the Busy Bee with a "Controlling Manager," or the Results Producer with a "True Leader"? Each of the work style combinations can help you recognize your strengths and weaknesses within a team. The suggested actions offer both the assistant and manager ways to create a more productive partnership.

Working With the Clueless Manager

The Desk Potato and the Clueless Manager

This pair faces a daunting challenge in trying to become a productive team. For one thing, in most cases, although both the manager and the assistant stumble along and manage to get things done, neither one has learned the communication skills necessary to make their partnership efficient and productive, let alone a smooth and easy interchange. As we have seen, the Desk Potato assistant seldom asks questions that will clarify what she is to do and why, and the Clueless Manager has trouble conveying what he wants or what takes priority. The two complete simple projects easily, but because both lack the ability to communicate effectively, misunderstandings occur and they are unable to complete more complicated tasks on time. Each identifies the other, of course, as the source of the problems they experience almost daily. For this pair to progress to a more productive working relationship, they must first be accountable for their actions and stop blaming each other or making excuses for their problems. A very simple first step in their case is to sit down and *talk!* The manager might think about checking in more to be sure the assistant understands his priorities and what results need to be produced. The assistant needs to ask more questions.

Here are some specific remedies this duo might try:

Desk Potato	Clueless Manager
• Learn to ask clarifying questions. • Schedule daily manager meetings to discuss priorities. • Take responsibility for results produced and not produced. • Learn to express needs and wants, practice better communication (see communication exercises in Chapter 9). • Take an assertiveness training course. • Ask for performance feedback on a regular basis.	• When making requests or providing information, be sure assistant understands what is being communicated and what is needed. • Give deadlines for all projects. • Take responsibility for actions that affect your assistant and team. • Clarify short- and long-term goals and objectives. • Define expectations. • Offer regular feedback.

The Busy Bee and the Clueless Manager

This combination often performs as a satisfactory team, mainly because the Busy Bee is such a hard worker. Because the Busy Bee always seems to have a million things to do, the Clueless Manager is unsure of when, where, and how to step in and establish priorities more in line with what projected goals demand. The Busy Bee prides herself on being a "good worker" and, because of this, the Clueless Manager worries about upsetting her routines or making her feel incompetent. The Busy Bee, in turn, is frustrated. She wants to ask for more time, more clarity, more direction, but she doesn't. The Clueless Manager is overwhelmed by the Busy Bee's seemingly uninterruptable activity and remains dissatisfied with what are clearly less than acceptable results. Both the Clueless Manager and the Busy Bee tend to think in terms of completing tasks rather than achieving overall results, which leads to miscommunication, frustration, and, eventually, blaming behavior.

To develop a successful partnering relationship, each side needs to accept responsibility for the breakdowns in communication, and both need to shift from a task orientation to a results orientation. Here are some steps that might prove useful:

Busy Bee	Clueless Manager
• Schedule regular manager meetings to discuss priorities.	• Focus assistant on priorities, and keep her informed.
• Show manager how best to utilize your skills.	• Focus on results, not tasks.
• Learn to say no when necessary and then negotiate.	• Take responsibility for actions that affect your assistant and team.
• Enroll in a time management course.	• Periodically check your assistant's workload.
• Ask for help more often.	• Define expectations for yourself and your assistant.
• Keep manager informed of completed tasks/results.	• Take a management training course.
• Schedule time to discuss career path.	

The Results Producer and the Clueless Manager

What happens when we pair up the Results Producer and the infamous Clueless Manager? Certainly not a highly compatible or productive team to start with, this duo does have the potential for becoming both. In this case, it is the Results Producer who must do most of the work. Obviously, the Clueless Manager seldom sees his shortcomings, or he would not be clueless, so the assistant, through her actions, must try to train her manager.

When the two sit down to talk, the assistant can be the one to raise questions about the larger picture and the long-range goals expected of both of them. (As we are beginning to see, scheduling regular meetings is a primary intervention for all scenarios being discussed here.) Once these goals are clear, the Results Producer verifies with the manager any intermediate steps to take and the expected results. In the process, the assistant clarifies priorities, and the manager determines any remaining questions that need answers. With regularly scheduled meetings, the Clueless Manager and the Results Producer can make significant gains.

The results-producing assistant, in most cases, is the one who must model what it means to communicate well, to resolve conflicts, and to create a productive team relationship. At least in the beginning, the Results Producer will have to ask for feedback on a regular basis to ensure that she is providing the results her manager wants and will have to let her manager know what she needs from her to do her job well. The two should use review time as an opportunity to communicate openly about their work styles and how they can best support each other.

Here are the steps that each can take to improve the work relationship and become part of an effective and productive team:

Results Producer	Clueless Manager
• Schedule regular meetings to review daily/weekly priorities • "Manage up" when appropriate. • Ask clarifying questions even when you know the bigger picture. • Enroll in a management-skills class. • Ask for feedback about the results you are producing.	• Keep meeting with your assistant. • Stay focused on results, not tasks. • Enroll in a management training course. • Find a mentor. • Ask your assistant for feedback.

Working With the Controlling Manager

The Desk Potato and the Controlling Manager

Now let's turn to a different pair with slightly different dynamics: the Desk Potato and the Controlling Manager. This combination experiences many challenges as they attempt to become a productive team. Neither has learned the communication skills needed to work together effectively. A Controlling Manager is a demanding manager who wants more and better and who insists on doing it her way. A Desk Potato, on the other hand, does not share one bit of her manager's intensity and perfectionist standards, so the struggle is on. The Desk Potato often responds to control-type people by digging in her heels and doing less rather than more. Some people would describe her behavior as "passive-aggressive." The ensuing breakdowns that occur each day make the controlling personality increasingly anxious. However, one common attribute of the Controlling Manager is his great concern for and his dedication to a high-quality product or service. The Desk Potato typically has a methodical approach to work that complements this manager's work style, allowing the team to complete many tasks. When constant interruptions and last-minute changes arise, the Desk Potato may slow down the work flow to ensure accuracy. This can be useful at times. People with these work styles need to acknowledge their differences and focus on their strengths to boost their confidence as a team. Here are some suggestions for doing this.

Desk Potato	Controlling Manager
• Schedule daily meetings. • Ask for direction regarding priorities. • Continually ask clarifying questions. • Ask manager to define expectations and goals. • Set weekly meetings to discuss performance.	• Focus your assistant on priorities, and keep her informed. • Keep scheduled meetings with your assistant. • Offer constructive and regular feedback regarding performance, and include positive action-oriented feedback. • Be aware of your tone of voice when speaking with your assistant (e.g., demanding, patronizing) (see Chapter 9). • Define expectations for yourself and your assistant.

The Busy Bee and the Controlling Manager

When a Busy Bee works with a Controlling Manager, the team typically works well for a while, even when they have communication breakdowns or when one partner is in crisis mode. There is great potential for this team of two to develop into a True Leader and a Results Producer as long as they don't focus on each other's weaknesses. Interestingly, they share the impulse to work harder and faster, and neither one stops to evaluate whether all of that activity is as purposeful and effective as it appears to be, at least in their minds. They do, however, manage to complete many tasks in a short period of time because their work styles enable them to work intensively and quickly. With a tendency for such a high-paced work flow, they spend a fair amount of time putting out fires caused by oversights and miscommunications, as in the case of Terry and Chris, introduced at the beginning of this chapter. If Controlling Managers and Busy Bees do not step back to reassess whether their actions directly lead them to their desired results, they can lose valuable time and productivity. Given this high-speed, intense team, it is likely that one or both will eventually burn out, move on to a better position, or quit.

These partners share a strong need to "look good" at all costs and to focus most of their energy on their own workloads. Their challenge is to focus on the team and not on their individual tasks and accomplishments. They need to develop stronger communication skills and to take more responsibility for their mistakes. Slowing the pace and paying more attention to the details will help reduce communications breakdowns. When these two give each other regular feedback and update priorities, they are able to develop a team that produces better results with less friction along the way. They need to reflect on how their work styles are undermining their productivity. For them, the remedies are:

Busy Bee	Controlling Manager
• Focus on solutions, not the problems/conflicts.	• Keep your assistant informed of changes regarding priorities.
• Slow down and ask clarifying questions.	• Keep scheduled meetings with your assistant.
• Meet regularly to clarify priorities before taking action.	• Offer constructive and regular feedback regarding performance, and include positive, action-oriented feedback.
• Assess and reassess "to do" list.	
• Ask for constructive and regular feedback regarding performance.	• Acknowledge your assistant for work well done.
• Inform manager immediately when feeling overwhelmed.	• Consider taking a stress management class.
• Focus on the results, not the tasks that need to be produced.	

The Results Producer and the Controlling Manager

If we give our Controlling Manager an assistant who is a Results Producer, what happens? This pair can, in fact, be a productive team in time, particularly as the manager comes to recognize the Results Producer's capabilities and feels confident that the assistant will get the job done. It is important that the Controlling Manager be supportive in the relationship, providing the information her assistant needs when she needs it, holding reasonable expectations, and giving clear feedback. On the other hand, because the Results Producer is dedicated to the job, highly competent, and a good communicator, if her manager should, under stress, revert to a strident, demanding mode, she will recognize it as a sign of anxiety and know how to deal with it. In her hands, major stumbling blocks are transformed into opportunities to clarify priorities. She knows how to ride gently over those speed bumps. With her anxiety relieved, the Controlling Manager gradually becomes more trusting. Before the relationship is cemented, however, some managers with a controlling nature may regard a skilled assistant as a threat, someone who wants to take over their job. When the manager knows the assistant has no such designs, she relaxes and can form part of a highly productive team. Once the Controlling Manager begins to see herself operating as a team with the Results Producer, she is well on her way to becoming a True Leader. And what does this pair need to achieve this lofty status? Let's look.

Results Producer	Controlling Manager
• Meet regularly to clarify priorities.	• Provide information on timely basis.
• Formulate a career path with your manager.	• Delegate more projects and responsibilities as appropriate.
• Ask for feedback regarding performance.	• Acknowledge your assistant for work well done.
• Inform your manager when you've created results.	• Consider taking a stress management class.
• Manage "up" or support your manager when necessary.	• Keep scheduled meetings.

Working With the True Leader

Looking at the three team combinations in which the True Leader is the managerial counterpart, it seems that anyone described as a True Leader should be able to work well with any assistant, as the Results Producer should be able to work with any manager regardless of work style. Well, yes and no. True Leaders enhance the productivity and effectiveness of and serves as role models for partners with any work style. They provide clear direction and motivate staff, including them in decision making and giving them constructive feedback on their performance. By definition, True Leaders are more than successful managers because they understand that there is always room for improvement. The list of leadership behaviors that contribute to a positive and productive partnership with any work style includes these qualities:

- Holds a clear vision of the company's mission and communicates it well.
- Defines expectations, roles, and responsibilities for assistant.
- Keeps commitments made to others.
- Practices effective communication.
- Listens with understanding.
- Includes assistant in goal setting.
- Codevelops assistant's career path and is committed to fostering assistant's professional growth.
- Motivates others with positive actions and behavior.
- Focuses on results.
- Shares information with assistant in a timely manner.
- Admits mistakes and offers solutions.
- Values and acknowledges assistant's contribution to the team.

Given these personal and professional characteristics, the True Leader is better able to develop productive partnerships with any assistant work style than are managers with other work styles. For one thing, integral to being a True Leader is having finely tuned interpersonal skills. On the other hand, True Leaders, as high performers with high performance standards, ultimately want their assistants to deliver the goods—to work productively at full potential. To achieve that goal, True Leaders must have assistants who, if not yet functioning at that level, are willing to develop themselves and be developed by the manager.

The Desk Potato and the True Leader

This team has the potential for becoming highly productive. Since the True Leader knows how to work with many different work styles and is able to communicate effectively and motivate others, she is able to provide the Desk Potato assistant with an opportunity to develop into a Results Producer. The Desk Potato who resists developing advanced skills to function more efficiently will eventually quit or lose her job.

In their work relationship, the True Leader needs first to pay attention to clarifying routinely her expectations of the assistant; then, as a person with a strong sense of future, she needs to inspire the Desk Potato to think beyond the task, to develop a career path, and to see who the work she does affects others.

This combination provides a perfect opportunity for the Desk Potato to increase knowledge and to learn new skills. It also gives the True Leader an opportunity to continue to fine-tune her leadership skills. These two can be a successful team if the Desk Potato learns to assume responsibility for her role and is proactive and innovative in achieving team goals. Some recommendations for this combo are:

Desk Potato	True Leader
• Check in daily to learn new priorities.	• Provide assistant with 6-month goals and objectives.
• Ask clarifying questions when unsure about results that need to be produced.	• Offer constructive and consistent feedback.
• Ask for regular feedback (set weekly meetings for this).	• Set clear priorities and explain the bigger picture.
• Enroll in an assertiveness class.	• Help assistant focus on results, not tasks.
• Compare "to do" list with manager's priorities.	• Keep scheduled meetings.

The Busy Bee and the True Leader

This pair can, in time, be a highly productive and successful team. The greatest challenge for the manager is keeping the Busy Bee on track, because of the Busy Bee's need to do, do, and do more. The greatest challenge for the Busy Bee is slowing down long enough to listen to the manager. The True Leader, of course, wants long-range results, not busywork. It is therefore up to the True Leader, at least in the beginning, to assure the Busy Bee of her value (which for her is systematically crossing out tasks on a long "to-do" list) and to encourage her to slow down, look at the big picture, and focus more on long-range results. The Busy Bee who learns to listen and take responsibility for all of her actions, will, in time, develop into a Results Producer.

To learn to work together, this pair should consider these ideas:

Busy Bee	True Leader
• Slow down and take purposeful actions.	• Provide assistant with specific priorities with due dates.
• Ask for regular feedback.	• Offer feedback regularly.
• Assess and reassess "to do" list before taking action.	• Set clear goals and career path.
• Schedule regular meetings with manager.	• Help assistant focus on results, not tasks.
• Focus on results, not tasks.	• Keep scheduled meetings.

The Results Producer and the True Leader

This partnership is obviously the one everyone strives for. It is attainable for any of the work style combinations. All it takes is a willingness to believe that high-level team functioning is possible as well as a commitment from both sides to work on building a productive partnership.

Developing this dynamic duo, however, does not happen overnight. By practicing the core competencies (see Chapters 5–9), assistants and managers can achieve a high-performance partnership that works smarter, not harder. The partners have clear expectations of their working relationship and have mutually agreed-upon boundaries. They both have career paths and support each other's professional growth. They are both focused on the same results, and they anticipate any barriers that might arise and address them together. Both are effective communicators and are responsible for their actions.

The challenge facing this pair is to be mentors for other manager-assistant teams. Here are the steps to keeping a productive partnership on track:

Results Producer	True Leader
• Keep scheduled meetings.	• Continue to provide information on a timely basis.
• Inform manager about barriers to producing results and suggest solutions.	• Delegate more projects and responsibilities as appropriate.
• Acknowledge manager's leadership abilities.	• Continue to offer feedback and acknowledgment.
• Continue to ask for feedback as needed.	• Take courses to improve leadership skills.
• Take appropriate courses that will improve skills.	• Keep scheduled meetings.

*   *   *   *   *

These work styles are tools for improving your productivity and your working relationship with your manager. They are not intended to make you feel bad about yourself if you aren't a Results Producer, or angry because your manager isn't a True Leader. Rather, these combinations can give you a way to measure your growth time.

In today's workplace, individual effort is often not enough; most businesses rely on teams in which each person has a specific contribution to make to the whole. Good communication among all of the players is essential to the success of these collaborations.

The key players in all companies are the manager and their assistant. Acknowledging that as assistants you are responsible for a different set of functions from those of your managers, it is nevertheless your ability to work with them, harmoniously and productively, that is essential to meeting—even exceeding— short- and long-range goals. As support staff, you are the "hub" communicators—at the center of things, constantly going back and forth relaying messages, requests for information, confirmations, queries, reports, schedules—who are essential if the company is to accomplish its goal of meeting its clients' needs.

In Part Two, we address the Five Core Competencies that Results Producers use in their daily work life. These tools will help you continually improve your working relationships and your job satisfaction.

Part Two
The Five Core Competencies

Chapter 4

Basic Training:
The Core Competencies

Being productive takes more than working hard or keeping busy. For assistants to become or continue to be results producers, they must learn and master a core set of skills and attitudes I call the Five Core Competencies. Those who practice these daily experience greater job satisfaction and higher productivity.

To better understand these Core Competencies, think about the alphabet. It is essential to know each letter before you can construct words, phrases, and sentences. Similarly, the Five Core Competencies are the basis for being a Results Producer. The Core Competencies go beyond what you ordinarily regard as your work skills—your computer expertise, keyboarding speed, organizational strengths, people skills, and so on. They are more fundamental; they have to do with your attitude toward work, your actions toward others, and, ultimately, your standards as a professional.

The Core Competencies are presented in Figure 4-1 in an A-B-C-D-E format. But unlike the A-B-C's, which become "invisible" in your daily life, these skills must be reviewed often if you are to be in command of your career and maintain your status as a Results Producer. They are:

A   Accountability
B   Belief that Barriers are opportunities, not obstacles
C   Commitment to results
D   Desire to learn
E   Effective communication

Figure 4-1. The Five Core Competencies.

Definitions of the Five Core Competencies

The core competencies may be defined in this way:

1. *Accountability.* This competency means taking 100 percent responsibility for your actions, *whether or not* you produced the intended result.
2. *Belief that barriers are opportunities rather than obstacles. Belief* means choosing not to let barriers stop you and seeing them as opportunities to find new ways to create the intended result; a *barrier* is defined as an interruption in the flow of work that can stop you from creating your intended result. Barriers crop up continually.

3. *Commitment to results.* This competency is defined as declaring your intention to create the desired results and taking all necessary actions to produce them.
4. *Desire to learn.* If you have this competency, you are looking for ways to improve your skills and invent more productive ways to create results.
5. *Effective communication.* This refers to the practice of ensuring the clarity of results, whether you are giving or receiving a communication.

In my conversations with CEOs and support staff from a variety of industries, these five core competencies emerged as the unspoken attributes that best describe (1) what employers value most in their assistants and (2) what successful and satisfied assistants consistently demonstrate in their work and work relationships.

The list is deceptively simple. You might read through it quickly and say, "Big deal—I've got those." In my experience, however, most breakdowns, conflicts, and job dissatisfaction can be traced back to a failure in one of these core disciplines. (When I speak of failure in this context, I do not mean a personal failure, which is how many of us define failures. I mean instead a work breakdown that could have been avoided or quickly remedied had one or more of these core competencies been applied.) Whenever you encounter a barrier, use the five competencies as a guide to help you determine what is in the way of success and what to anticipate or prevent the next time.

In today's changing work environment, assistants are expected to "hit the ground running," competently fulfilling an expanded set of complex responsibilities. Most assistants are not professionally trained to do the challenging work of an assistant. Because of this, many lack the knowledge and skills needed to take charge of the various challenges and barriers that arise, making it more difficult to gain real satisfaction from the daily tasks.

U.S. businesses are in a period of rapid change; companies have consolidated, downsized, restructured, or jumped into new arenas to be part of the new global marketplace. Because of this, job descriptions are more flexible than ever before, and fewer restrictions are being placed on what is and can be asked of workers at all levels and in a variety of professions. The cryptic line "other duties as assigned" is now a standard part of most job descriptions.

While this new "elasticity" sometimes feels like a boomerang that hits you right in the face, it can also mean increased opportunities for those willing to take on the challenge. Now more than ever, you need to cultivate a set of skills that can take you anywhere you want to go—even if "anywhere you want to go" means holding onto the job you've already got!

Complete the assessment on the following pages before moving on to the next five chapters, in which I will explain the core competencies in greater detail and offer practical exercises and suggestions for how to implement them on a daily basis.

Assessing Your Productivity Using the Five Core Competencies

The worksheet in this section is designed to help you assess your current level of productivity by evaluating your use of the Five Core Competencies at work. Assessing your productivity is the first step to discovering new ways to improve your job performance and your job satisfaction.

This assessment will benefit you most if you do the following:

1. Set aside undisturbed time to complete the questionnaire without interruption. (Allow approximately ten minutes.)
2. Answer with your first response.
3. Answer each item truthfully.

Remember, as with any assessment, its real value comes from being totally honest with yourself. It is not about trying to get a high score. It is about seeing an accurate evaluation regarding the Five Core Competencies—which then allows for improvement and professional growth, Otherwise, you are just fooling yourself.

Also, this assessment is a great tool for measuring your growth in these areas by taking it again at a later date.

(*text continues on page 56*)

Worksheet 2:
Assessing Your Productivity

Instructions:

Read each statement and put a number from 1 to 7 in the box located to the right of the statement. Total the numbers in each column (A-E) at the bottom of each page. Put the total from each column at the end of the worksheet. Each column should have a number ranging from 10 to 70. If you have a number greater than 60 in any column (A–E), go back and re-add each column from each page. Once you have your scores, refer to the section "Understanding Your Scores" to find out what they mean.

Scale

1 —— 2 —— 3 ——3.5—— 4 —— 5 —— 6 —— 7
Almost never   50% of the Time   Almost Always

	A	B	C	D	E
I ask my manager to clarify his/her expectations of me. _____	☐				
When a crisis happens at work (e.g., fax or copier breaks down), I enjoy the challenge of resolving it. _____		☐			
I take classes/workshops to improve my knowledge/skills for my job. _____				☐	
I am clear about the primary mission, goals, and objectives of my company. _____			☐		
When I ask a coworker to do work for me, I ask if she has any questions about what results I expect. _____					☐
TOTAL					

1 —— 2 —— 3 ——3.5—— 4 —— 5 —— 6 —— 7
Almost never   50% of the Time   Almost Always

Statement	A	B	C	D	E
When a new project comes up, I check my workload first before volunteering to be a part of it.	☐				
I examine standard work procedures to look for more efficient ways to do work.				☐	
I solve problems rather than complain about them.		☐			
When I receive a request, I ask questions until I am absolutely clear about what result is expected of me.					☐
I let my manager know when we are off-track in our meetings.			☐		
I have someone at work that I consider my mentor.				☐	
When I realize that I don't have the skills I need to do my work, I ask for help or training.		☐			
I have received awards for work well done, both in my current job and in past jobs.			☐		
I attend staff meetings and read literature and newspapers to keep apprised of the latest happenings at my company.	☐				
I create solutions to keep problems from happening over and over again.		☐			
I look for skills I can learn to improve my value to my company.				☐	
TOTAL					

1 — 2 — 3 —3.5— 4 — 5 — 6 — 7
Almost never   50% of the Time   Almost Always

	A	B	C	D	E
The results I create in my job affect my manager's ability to create his results.			☐		
Whenever my manager makes a new request of me, I ask questions until I am absolutely clear about the results he/she wants me to create.	☐				
I state my purpose in all communications that I initiate.					☐
When I make a request of others, I ask them to repeat the result to be produced.					☐
I give my undivided attention when I am in conversation with my manager.					☐
I do informational interviews with people in my company whose jobs I find interesting.				☐	
I meet with my manager daily (via phone or in person) to see what additional support he/she needs.			☐		
I look for potential problems and take action to keep them from happening.		☐			
I ask for help when I don't know how to do something.				☐	
I am clear about the purpose of all meetings I attend.			☐		
I expect problems to happen in my job.		☐			
When I make a mistake, I readily admit it.	☐				
TOTAL					

1 —— 2 —— 3 ——3.5—— 4 —— 5 —— 6 —— 7
Almost never   50% of the Time   Almost Always

Statement	A	B	C	D	E
When someone initiates a communication with me, I ask questions to understand the purpose of our conversation.					☐
I solicit feedback from my manager regarding my job performance.	☐				
I enjoy looking for ways to improve my job.				☐	
Before I make a request of someone, I am absolutely clear about what specific result I need.					☐
I exhaust all available resources before I bring a problem to my manager.		☐			
I manage my projects to completion.			☐		
My manager and I meet daily to update each other.	☐				
I am absolutely clear about the results I am to produce in my job.			☐		
I enjoy working in a constantly changing environment.				☐	
I keep my mind from wandering when I am in a conversation with my manager or coworker.					☐
I go to my manager for help and/or support when I need it.		☐			
TOTAL					

	A	B	C	D	E
1 — 2 — 3 —3.5— 4 — 5 — 6 — 7 Almost never / 50% of the Time / Almost Always					
When my manager misses a meeting, I hold myself responsible. _____	☐				
I communicate clearly with my manager and coworkers to positively effect the results we create. _____					☐
I take the initiative with my manager, asking for updates and giving him a progress report. _____	☐				
When I say yes, I mean that I will do something no matter what, not that I will just try. _____			☐		
I enjoy the challenge of doing work I have never done before. _____				☐	
I know what I want to achieve from each conversation I initiate. _____					☐
I ask my coworkers for their expertise and input when working on a new project. _____				☐	
I follow up with others who do not keep their promises to me and ask for a new promise. _____			☐		
I don't get frustrated or annoyed when problems arise in my work. _____		☐			
I hold myself responsible for my job satisfaction. _____	☐				
TOTAL					

DIRECTIONS: Insert the totals for this page. Turn the page and add totals from this and the previous pages.

Refer to the next section for a brief explanation of your scores in each section (A, B, C, D, E).

Total from page 51
Total from page 52
Total from page 53
Total from page 54
Total from page 55
GRAND TOTAL

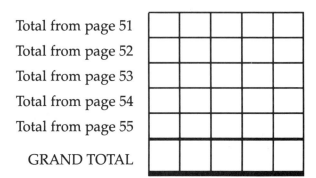

Understanding Your Scores

A = Accountability

60–70: You consider yourself responsible for helping your manager and your company to satisfy clients. You take full responsibility for your actions whether or not they are effective. When your actions are ineffective, you do what is necessary to correct them and move on to produce expected results.

Use Chapter 5 to help a coworker increase her level of accountability.

36–59: You consider yourself responsible for creating results for your manager but may not see how your efforts affect the overall success or failure of your company. You don't always take full responsibility for your actions, especially when they are ineffective. You sometimes offer stories or excuses to explain why you did not produce an expected result.

Refer to Chapter 5 to see how to increase your level of accountability. Be sure to complete the exercise. By being more accountable, you will increase your productivity and feel more in control and proud of your work.

10–35: You take many actions at work but don't hold yourself fully responsible for creating intended results. You don't take responsibility for your actions, especially when they are ineffective. You often offer excuses or stories or blame others when you don't produce results.

Carefully read Chapter 5 several times, and complete the exercise in it. This will help you increase your level of accountability, gain control of your work, and take pride in it.

B = Belief That Barriers Are Opportunities

60–70: You understand that problems are a natural occurrence at work and expect them. You take the actions necessary to anticipate and resolve problems that threaten to keep you from completing projects on time.

Use Chapter 6 to help a coworker learn to anticipate and resolve problems better.

36–59: You usually recognize problems when they occur but don't always respond productively to them. As a result, you sometimes let problems stop you from creating the results expected by your manager or coworkers.

Read the Chapter 6, and complete the exercise in it. This will help you to see how to respond to barriers more productively.

10–35: You tend to distance yourself from problems to avoid looking bad, doing extra work, or being seen as incompetent. As a result, you typically let problems stop you from creating results. If this continues over time, you run the risk of losing your job.

Carefully read Chapter 6 several times, and complete the exercise it contains. Companies value problem solvers, not problem avoiders. Learning to accept barriers as normal and to respond to them productively is key to producing results and, believe it or not, to enjoying work.

C = Commitment

60–70: You take your promises at work seriously. You make sure you are clear about the results expected of you, and you consistently take the actions necessary to follow projects through to completion. Refer to Chapter 7 to help a coworker learn to be more committed in their job.

36–59: You usually follow projects through to completion but don't always take all the actions necessary to guarantee your success. On occasion, you let lack of clarity or planning or other problems keep you from producing results on time. When this happens, you may offer excuses or stories to explain your ineffectiveness.

Read Chapter 7 for suggestions on how to produce intended results consistently. Also, pay special attention to Phase 8 of the Productivity Cycle™ (see Chapter 13). Make sure to complete all exercises in both chapters.

0–35: You don't take the actions necessary to complete projects on time. You typically plan ineffectively and let problems get in the way of creating expected results. You usually offer excuses or stories and blame others to explain your ineffectiveness at creating results.

Carefully read Chapters 7 and 13 several times. Complete all exercises in both chapters. Learning to be committed to intended results in essential to your job success.

D = Desire to Learn

60–70: You look for opportunities to improve the work you do for your manager, coworkers, and company. You are willing to learn new skills when necessary to increase your value to yourself and to your company.

Read Chapter 8 and use it to help a coworker or friend see the benefits of learning for himself and for his company.

36–59: You are willing to innovate in your job and learn new skills, but you don't assertively find ways to do so. You are sometimes hesitant to ask for help or to request training because it requires you to expose your incompetence or inefficiencies.

Read Chapter 8, and complete the exercise in it. Learning gives you the opportunity to increase your competence and therefore your value to yourself and your company.

10–35: You are most comfortable when performing job responsibilities you are familiar with. You usually don't seek ways to improve your job or learn new skills unless asked to do so. You prefer the status quo.

Carefully read Chapter 8 several times, and complete the exercises in it. Learning new skills can increase your self-confidence and make you more valuable to your company.

E = Effective Communication

60–70: You understand the important connection between communicating effectively and producing results. You take full responsibility for the clarity of the communications you engage in, whether as speaker or as listener. This helps you to produce expected results consistently.

Read Chapter 9 and the Productivity Cycle™ chapters. Teach a coworker to become a more effective communicator using the Productivity Cycle™.

36–59: You need to be clearer in your communications (whether you are speaking or listening) with others. When making or receiving requests, make sure you and others are clear about what is wanted. Read Chapter 9 and the Productivity Cycle™ chapters, and complete the exercises in them. This will help you to see how you can interact more effectively with your manager and your coworkers to produce results.

10–35: You do not communicate with your manager and your coworkers in a way that ensures the production of desired results. You don't listen usually attentively or ask the questions necessary to clarify unclear requests.

Carefully read Chapter 9 and the Productivity Cycle™ chapters, and complete the exercises in them. This will help you to see how you can interact more effectively with your manager and your coworkers to produce results.

Chapter 5
The Buck Stops Here: Accountability

As the first and most fundamental Core Competency, accountability is critical to any assistant's job performance and satisfaction. Accountability means taking 100 percent responsibility for what you say and for the actions you take, whether or not you produce the results. This chapter provides tools for measuring the level of accountability and practical exercises to develop new levels of ownership on the job.

1. Accountability Helps You Learn

When I was working for a consulting company many years ago and training another assistant to do my job, we got our wires crossed at one point—we both thought the other had taken care of scheduling a meeting between John, the president, whom I supported, and one of his biggest clients. When John asked about the time and place of that meeting, we reacted by pointing fingers at each other, neither of us wanting to take responsibility for our actions.

After realizing that the way we were dealing with the situation was getting us nowhere, we decided to simply tell John that we had made a mistake, and let him know what we had done to ensure that it wouldn't happen a second time. We even brought in bagels and lox, because he had once said, "Celebrate mistakes"; he believed that mistakes were opportunities for improvement, so we took him at his word.

I relay this story not to make light of the mistake we made—it could have cost one of us our job—but to emphasize that accountability starts with your willingness to give up blaming, hiding, and not telling the complete truth and instead accept the consequences of your actions. Acknowledging mistakes is a more professional behavior, and in the workplace it can only enhance your power and respectability.

It can help you understand the concept of accountability if you consider how you personally contribute to events and situations in your life, both professionally and personally. Take a moment to reflect on several of the events currently in the forefront of your own life (i.e., the fight you had with a friend this morning, the promotion you got last week, the difficulties you have working with your manager, your failure to create an important result for your work team, the project you completed by the due date). Consider these situations and events from two standpoints: (1) as if you contributed to them, and (2) as if they *just happened to you.*

When you look at the events as if they just happened to you, you see yourself as always being victimized by someone or something else, whether the events are positive or negative. When positive events occur (i.e., you're given a pay raise), you typically don't acknowledge the fact that you had something to do with the outcome. Instead, you attribute it to luck, another person, or to some other external factor beyond your control. When negative events happen, you often assume the role of victim, blaming someone or something else for "doing it to you" or keeping you from creating your results. You do not, or are not willing to, see or acknowledge how you personally have contributed to the situation for fear that you or others will see you as a failure. When you look at your life and the world in this way, you often feel angry, righteous, resentful, resigned, anxious, or powerless.

Think back to the last time you were really annoyed or frustrated with your manager. What happened to make you annoyed or frustrated? What did you think about your manager at the time? How did you react? Often the automatic reaction is to do whatever you can to make the other person responsible for the situation at hand—in other words, to blame the person. Usually, you are convinced that you are "right" and the other person is "wrong."

On the other hand, when you look at events as if you contributed to them, you can see clearly how you personally and professionally affect the events or situations in your worklife and are willing to acknowledge this contribution openly, to yourself and to others. You need to learn to accept confidently and graciously feedback, positive or negative.

Taking full responsibility for an event or situation tends to be easiest when the event is positive. Typically, people enjoy taking the credit for such events and often feel proud, successful, excited, and happy about the outcomes of their actions. Think, for example, about the last time you produced a positive result that was acknowledged by your manager or your work team. How did you feel about creating this result? Chances are you enjoyed the experience and felt good about it.

When people are involved in events or situations that they initially perceive as negative, they tend to deny their parts in the events because they fear they will look bad or incompetent. That is the last perception people want to give to their managers or coworkers. In addition, people simply don't see how they might have contributed to the perceived negative outcome. When you assume full responsibility for such events, it allows you to see when and how your actions have been ineffective and what new actions you can take now and in the future. When you do this, you have shifted your paradigm.

Figure 5-1 illustrates possible responses to an event from an accountable and an unaccountable stance. For each event, people have choices about what stance they are going to take. It's best to acknowledge mistakes immediately and take steps to ensure that the initial error is not compounded by more mistakes and more backlash from coworkers. If you pass the buck, eventually it will be passed back to you.

After looking at Figure 5-1, think again about the time when you were annoyed or frustrated with your manager. Now take a moment and ask yourself the following questions: What role did you play in the situation? How could you have responded differently? How might this response have created a better outcome? In the following case study Judy was stuck in an unpro-

Figure 5-1. Choosing How We Respond to Events.

ductive paradigm about her work relationship with her manager because of her lack of accountability.

Judy, a bright woman in her late thirties, stood up at one of my training sessions and said, "My boss never gives me the time of day." It seems that she frequently needed to get information from him, but whenever she approached him, he had something more pressing to do. She even tried scheduling herself on his calendar, but that didn't work either. She became increasingly frustrated and then downright angry. She started going to coworkers and other managers to find out what she needed to know to do her job, but she remained very resentful of her boss's behavior and attitude.

I asked her whether she could take a look to see how she might be contributing to this situation. At first, she didn't understand my question. I then asked whether there might be another way to approach him so that he would be more open and willing to sit down with her. Naturally, she said she had tried everything and that the problem was really all his. She had done her part.

I continued to probe. Had she considered such things as her timing? Her tone of voice? The words she used when she approached him? She acknowledged that she hadn't. We explored what being accountable meant in her situation, and she began to open up. It soon came out that she had little respect for him. We were then able to talk about how lack of respect for another is often fueled by lack of respect for ourselves. In Judy's case, she finally acknowledged that she allowed her manager to use excuses to avoid having meetings. She also recognized her unwillingness to confront him, even though it was ultimately for his benefit. Did she shift her paradigm about her work relationship with her manager? How?

Judy called me after going back to her job to tell me that she finally had had a conversation with her manager about the need to meet more regularly, stressing that the meetings would benefit him. Together, they agreed to meet for twenty minutes twice a week. This may not have been Judy's ideal, but at least she was able to meet with him. More important, she took accountability for getting her needs met to do the best job she is capable of. This resulted in increased productivity and greater job satisfaction.

The only behavior you can change is your own. In the example, Judy had to take a risk and sit down with her manager and tell him in a way he could hear that it was important for them to meet regularly. Typically, people say that it's the managers' responsibility to give them the information they need to do their jobs, so the managers should make the time for necessary meetings. This may be true, but it's beside the point. Each of you has to take accountability for you own behavior and attitude.

When you begin to accept accountability for your actions, people will notice. Your new behaviors, actions, and attitudes will affect others that you work with, particularly your manager. Real satisfaction comes when you decide to stop "renting" your job and "own" it, instead. Without making that (paradigm) shift in your relationship to your work, you will continue to experience frequent breakdowns, nonproductive time, mediocre to just satisfactory performance reviews, low motivation to get up in the morning, and far less satisfaction than you could have and deserve to have.

Accountability is only a nice concept until you put it into daily practice. The easiest way to do this is to understand how accountability looks in terms of behavior and attitudes at work. What does it really mean to take 100 percent responsibility for what you say and for your actions? Sometimes it works to say what something is *not* as a way of arriving at what it *is*. Being accountable, in addition to not blaming, means not dodging, defending, evading, avoiding, or flat-out lying, all of which are hopelessly unproductive ways of dealing with barriers (we discuss this more in Chapter 6). When there are others involved in any activity, it is often tempting to point to what they did or did not do, is especially when a breakdown or failure is involved. (If everything turns out right in the end, no one cares or remembers who might have dropped the ball along the way.)

Accountability is a tool for producing the results you are paid for at work. Do not use it to become a victim or to put others in the wrong. Sometimes when people are learning about accountability, they take it to the extreme and assume other people's mistakes as their own, even to the point of martyrdom. This is not what accountability is about. Practicing accountability is being able to know when it is appropriate to delegate and ensuring that the other person knows exactly what you need them to do. It is also knowing when to ask for help to make sure the result will be produced. Accountability does not give you the right to blame someone whom you perceive as not being responsible or owning his contribution of the breakdown. If you choose to engage in this ineffective behavior, know that it will work only for a short time and that eventually it will tire coworkers and management, resulting in an unproductive and unsatisfying job. Blaming is a useless behavior with no productive purpose. It arouses bad feelings and creates unproductive and sometimes defensive behavior. When you blame yourself or others, you open the door to a destructive vicious cycle.

Accountability isn't about saying, "It's all my fault." It offers an opportunity to see how you contribute to the events in your life and to take actions to create change when you are resentful, dissatisfied, or unproductive.

Being accountable means "owning" the job, not just the parts you excel at or enjoy. It means having the leadership ability to look calmly at what broke down along the way, rather than who dropped the ball. It means having the confidence to stand up to interrogation, your own and that of others, and to accept the consequences.

Taking Accountability in the Workplace

Being accountable requires that you separate the person from the action. It is so easy simply to criticize yourself when you make a mistake. However, when you respect yourself and hold yourself in unshakably high esteem (yes, it's possible), mistakes and failures really do become opportunities. (Don't forget that to be truly accountable means acknowledging your effectiveness as well as your mistakes.)

When you know you've made a mistake and don't publicly acknowledge it, it occupies your mind and makes it impossible for you to be productive. Instead, you spend your time wondering if others will find out about the mistake and what they will think of you if they do.

The next time you make a mistake, try this simple exercise. Tell someone as soon as it happens, and brainstorm with that person about how you can avoid repeating it. This will immediately relieve the stress you feel when you keep your concern to yourself. It is equally important that you give yourself credit whenever you accomplish or achieve your desired outcome.

Unless you grew up in a Brady Bunch family (and some of

you did), you may not have learned the joys and pains of taking responsibility for your actions. Many people move into their adult years still firmly convinced that things "just happened" to them or that other people "did it" to them and that if not for these nasty twists of fate, they would be successful. The good news is that being accountable is something you can learn. With practice, you will find it's an easy way to attain greater satisfaction on the job and experience higher productivity.

To assess your accountability, look at Figure 5-2. Each quadrant represents a different view of accountability. Take a moment to review each quadrant, and then check each box that applies to you. Then which quadrant contains the most check marks.

Figure 5-2. The Accountability Matrix.

	ACCOUNTABLE	UNACCOUNTABLE
	Competent	**Low Self-Esteem**
POSITIVE RESULTS (Produced the intended result.)	❑ Confirm client satisfaction. ❑ See how your actions and attitudes created the result. ❑ Acknowledge yourself for work well done. ❑ Feel proud and successful (satisfied). ❑ Acknowledge others for their help when appropriate.	❑ Consider yourself lucky. ❑ Acknowledge others but not yourself for creating the result. ❑ Don't really see how your actions contributed to the end result. ❑ Doubt your own competence. ❑ See your effort as just part of the job.
	Responsible	**Destructive**
NEGATIVE RESULTS (Did not produce the intended result.)	❑ Acknowledge to yourself and others that you did not create the result. ❑ Focus on solution (take new actions to create the result). ❑ Look at what you can do differently next time. ❑ Consider mistakes a learning experience. ❑ Own your part of the result.	❑ See yourself as a victim. ❑ Blame others or situations for not producing results. ❑ Don't acknowledge how your own actions and attitudes keep you from creating the result. ❑ Feel angry/resentful. ❑ Don't see how your own actions and attitudes kept you from creating result (blind).
	PRODUCTIVE	**UNPRODUCTIVE**

Although many people have check marks in all four quadrants of Figure 5-2, some of you will see a pattern in your responses. Over the years, I have assessed more than a thousand assistants on the Five Core Competencies, and 94 percent of the participants scored the lowest in the area of Accountability. In fact, my research showed that a lack of accountability was the number one reason for lowered productivity. How can you be really productive if you are spending your time and energy blaming yourself or someone else for breakdowns, conflicts, problems, and mistakes? Learning to accept accountability takes the willingness to face yourself with warmth and compassion and the desire to shed old ways or patterns that no longer work. If you can do this and want to change, you can accomplish remarkable outcomes. For an example, let's look at the case of Terry and Chris.

A Study in Accountability

Remember the case study of Terry and Chris from Chapter 1? Here they are again, experiencing more difficulty.

Chris is once again overwhelmed because her manager, Terry, is making multiple, unrelated requests of her. She must juggle her priorities very frequently to accommodate conflicting deadlines, schedule changes, and other unplanned needs. Chris is finding it increasingly difficult to respond to work requests that must be accomplished within a short period of time. Her long-term projects remain in the 'Z' basket (the basket that never gets touched), making it more and more challenging to stay motivated and clear about the constantly changing priorities. Even more frustrating, Terry does not give Chris all the information she needs to set priorities until there is a crisis, making it impossible for Chris to complete her work on time. Chris finds herself in this situation time and time again, and as a result her productivity is declining. Terry is concerned about this but does not know what to do.

In the beginning, the lack of communication and the distrust between Terry and Chris growing out of their different work styles were contributing to their lack of accountability. When Terry did not take the time to communicate the purpose, needs, and priorities of Chris's tasks and projects and Chris did not clarify these points either, neither of them could hold the other accountable for her actions. When neither Terry nor Chris assumed individual responsibility for clear, honest communication, they both contributed to a system of poor accountability. Chris failed to accept accountability because she did not (1) clarify the top priorities, (2) inquire about the bigger picture so that she understood how her actions contributed to the large whole, or (3) ask about deadline changes, particularly on long-term projects. Chris was also not accountable for her actions when she said yes but needed to say no to additional work. She should have been honest about what she could reasonably accomplish. Furthermore, it was Chris's responsibility when she did say no to sort out her priorities. She could have said, "I can't take on an additional project right now because I'm working on the report for the meeting next week. If this project is the highest priority, I will do it; however, I will need help to get everything prepared for next week's meeting. In fact, I can ask Susan to work on the report with me. Does that work for you?" This statement would have clarified Chris's need to prioritize and informed Terry what could be rearranged in order to produce the results she wanted. Chris could also have offered to complete the request at a later time, or she could have recommended that someone else complete the project. Finally, it was Chris's responsibility to ask if her work was satisfactory and was meeting Terry's needs.

Now let's take a look at how Terry was also not being accountable for the breakdowns she was experiencing with Chris. Terry did not ensure that Chris understood what the top priorities were. It was Terry's responsibility to communicate the purpose of tasks and projects to Chris, as well as to provide her with the bigger picture; Terry's job includes making time to meet with Chris on a regular basis and let her know whether deadlines have changed. Terry needed to provide timely feedback to Chris, including expressing appreciation for work well done, and clear messages about what areas need improvement.

Even though Terry was not practicing accountability, this did not give Chris permission to avoid it. This was not the time to say, "Well, my manager isn't acting accountable, so why

Figure 5-3. Tips for Becoming Accountable.

When dealing with a situation or event that is perceived to be negative, ask yourself these three questions:

1. How did I contribute to this outcome?
2. What could I have done differently?
3. Is there a way or ways to prevent this from occurring again?

In addition to asking questions, here are some suggested actions to practice accountability:

1. Own your part in the success or breakdown of a result.
2. Speak up when you see problems or have concerns about creating results at work.
3. Ask questions when you are not clear about the results your manager has asked you to produce.
4. Ask for help when you know you need it.

should I?" You cannot let your manager's or coworkers behavior affect your ability to be professional and productive. This will only hurt you in the long run. If everyone contributes all she can to create the result, the likelihood that the result will get produced is much greater than if everyone concentrates on only her own piece. You must be willing to set an example for others by practicing accountability. The challenge will be to avoid slipping back into pointing the finger when the team doesn't produce the result.

Returning to Chris and Terry, their work relationship is suffering and productivity is declining because of their lack of accountability. Let's see what happens when Chris takes the initiative.

After weeks of stress, Chris finally takes a risk and approaches Terry. She asks to schedule a meeting about their work relationship. Terry agrees, because things certainly haven't been working for her. Both are a little nervous but are willing to make their relationship work. Chris starts by telling Terry that she hasn't been able to keep up with the changing and last-minute requests and that work is not getting done. She recognizes that she should have said something sooner, but she was worried about what Terry would think of her. Terry responds by acknowledging that she knew something was wrong, but she was too busy to ask Chris about it. She was waiting for Chris to come to her. She realizes that this has made the situation worse. Because both don't want this confusion to recur, they agree to check in with each other more frequently. If Chris is feeling overwhelmed or confused, she will tell Terry immediately. Terry reprioritizes Chris's workload and agrees to give her more timely feedback. Both walk away from the meeting reenergized about their work relationship and their ability to work as a team.

Now that we've assessed the work relationship between Chris and Terry, it is time to review our own accountability within your work relationships. Try following exercises in Worksheet 3 to assess your accountability regarding your job satisfaction, your ability to produce results, and your work relationships. See also Figure 5-3.

Worksheet 3: Assessing Your Accountability

1. Briefly describe a situation at work in which you produced a desired result for which you felt accountable.

   _____

   _____

   a. What was your specific contribution to creating the result(s)?

   _____

   _____

   b. How did you feel about your contribution?_____

   _____

   _____

2. List three areas regarding your work relationship that could be improved. _____

_____

_____

3. For each of these areas, answer the following questions:

   a. On a scale of 1 percent to 100 percent, how accountable are you for this area? _____

   _____

   _____

   b. If your answer to *a* was less than 100 percent, what is keeping you from being 100 percent accountable? _____

   _____

   _____

   c. What new actions can you take to be 100 percent accountable for improving this area? _____

   _____

   _____

   ### Summary: Being Accountable

   - Pay attention to the various situations and events in your life.
     —Know which events you are satisfied with.
     —Know which events you are dissatisfied with.
   - Notice how you personally contribute to each of the events and situations in your life, whether positive or negative.
   - Recognize the positive contributions you make to yourself and to others.

- Recognize when your attitudes and actions are ineffective and keep you from creating the results you desire.
- Recreate positive events for yourself and for others in the future.
- Turn negative contributions into positive ones.
- Become a stronger, more committed team player.
- Develop solution-minded approaches to problems.
- Invent new and better ways to create results.
- Control your own job satisfaction.

Practicing accountability isn't easy or comfortable at first. With time, however, it will become both, and the rewards will far outweigh the short-term discomfort.

Chapter 6

You've Gotta Believe: Barriers Are Opportunities

At work, we are paid to produce results. The actions we take and the conversations we have are all aimed at producing results that are of value to our companies. No matter how carefully we work, situations unavoidably arise that can keep us from creating the results we intend. Many of us perceive these challenges as barriers.

> *A barrier is an interruption in the flow of work that can stop you (if you let it) from producing the results you intend. And a belief as it relates to barriers is the ability to see that barriers are opportunities to improve the way you do your work. Figure 6-1 lists the most common.*

There are two common types of barriers that we've all encountered on the job—problems and conflicts.

What Is a Problem?

A problem is a situation or event that a person judges or perceives to be wrong or as needing to be "fixed." That something is perceived to be a problem by one person does not guarantee that it will be seen that way by another person. The person who perceives the situation or event as a problem is the person who is accountable for solving it. People are not problems, but their actions may create problems. At I mentioned in Chapter 5, it's

Figure 6-1. Common Barriers.

---

*In looking at these barriers, consider which are problems
and which are conflicts.*

✍ **UNEXPECTED SITUATIONS.**
EXAMPLE: The copier breaks down in the middle of an
urgent project.

✍ **LACK OF SPECIFIC SKILL(S)** needed to create an intended result.
EXAMPLE: You are unfamiliar with a new software program
that you need to produce a report.

✍ **LACK OF TIME** needed to produce an intended result.
EXAMPLE: Deadline has been moved up three hours.

✍ **FAILURE TO PRACTICE THE CORE COMPETENCIES.**
EXAMPLE: Lack of accountability for commitment to result.

✍ **MISTAKES** (Human Error).
EXAMPLE: You fax a confidential document to the wrong client.

✍ **COUNTERPRODUCTIVE MOODS/DIFFICULT PEOPLE.**
EXAMPLE: Anger, resignation, panic, distrust.

✍ **LACK OF INFORMATION.**
EXAMPLE: Manager doesn't give you the figures you need to
complete a report.

✍ **LACK OF AUTHORITY.**
EXAMPLE: You are unable to finalize travel plans for your
manager.

---

important to separate the person from the behavior. It is impossible to "fix" other people, although many people have tried. Furthermore, it is not your responsibility to "fix" the people in your life. However, it is your responsibility to solve the problems that you perceive to be getting in the way of your productivity. Some barriers are simple; the fax machine breaks down, or the boss is unavailable. Other barriers are more subtle; the work flow may be unnecessarily complicated; computer problems may occur; there may be no systems of checks and balances or tracking system, other people may not produce results in the time they promised. Figure 6-1 lists the most common barriers that assistants encounter in their daily work.

These are the most common barriers that assistants face every day:

- *Unexpected situations.* Your manager asks you to reproduce forty sales reports for the staff meeting set to begin in fifteen minutes. When you go to the copy machine, you find it is broken and will not be fixed for two hours. How would you solve this problem?
- *Lack of specific skills.* You manager leaves an urgent request for you via voice mail asking you to produce a special business report by 9:00 A.M. tomorrow morning, using Excel Software. You've never used this program before. How do you solve this problem? (Reminder: Think long term.)
- *Lack of time.* You have promised to produce a report for one of your coworkers by the end of the day. Your manager comes to you with two emergency projects that absolutely must be finished by the end of the work day. You do not have time to complete all three projects to the standards required. How do you solve this?
- *Human mistakes.* Your manager asks you to fax a project status report to a client in preparation for a conference call tomorrow morning at 10 A.M. You fax the report to the client and leave for the day. When you arrive at the office the next morning, you are informed that you faxed the report to the wrong number. How do you handle this problem?
- *Change in company policy or procedure.* Your manager is on a business trip overseas. He is available by telephone but only at four-day intervals. While he is gone, the accounting department announces a new travel reimbursement policy. Any expenses without original receipts attached to the travel report will not be reimbursed. You are aware that your manager pays little attention to saving receipts; until now, this has not presented a serious problem. What do you do?

Every assistant faces each of these barriers at one time or another. How they get solved varies according to each assistant's past experiences, work style, and work relationship with her manager. In each of the examples I have presented, there is an opportunity to solve the problem productively, keeping the long term in mind.

Let's take Lack of Specific Skills. This is a great opportunity to learn a new software program, Excel, yet it is impossible to learn it well enough to produce the report in the time your manager needs it. The short-term solution is to ask a coworker who is an expert in Excel if she will produce the report, since it won't take her very long. The long-term solution is either to ask your coworker if you can sit with her while she produces the report, taking notes, and then to schedule another time to practice or to enroll in an Excel class immediately so that the next time your manager asks you to produce a report you'll know how.

Barriers can be opportunities if you choose to see them as a way to learn, grow, or change. It's not about saying, "Okay, great, another breakdown"; rather, it is a chance to see how you can do things differently. When barriers come up, it's really hard to see the positive outcome; you're just trying to fix things as quickly as possible. Yet it has been my experience as an assistant that the most important question is, "Is this the best solution for the long term?" If you don't ask this question, then the problem is probably going to repeat itself. Most people know this and yet don't seem to learn from it. They tend to get caught up in whatever is happening in the moment and choose the easy solution so that they can move onto the next problem. Given all that they're expected to do each day, it's no wonder. However, if they continue to act in this way, they'll eventually become overwhelmed, panicked, and often resentful at having to deal with the same problems over and over.

The good news is that you can make a significant difference in this area for yourself and for your manager if you start looking past the short-term "band-aid" approach that many of you learned from past and current managers. When you stop—literally—and ask "What is the best solution for this problem?," then you can begin to cut down on the number of minifires that you'll have to put out. You'll also save yourself time and reduce anxiety and stress, thereby increasing your productivity. Managers appreciate solutions that will ultimately be cost-effective, so take the time initially and find the best long-term solution, which may require seeking information from coworkers about their jobs, tasks, and solutions.

Perception is the key to determining whether there is a problem or a breakdown. Problems are in the eyes of the beholder. Two people can see the same situation very differently; one can see it as a problem and the other can see it as an opportunity for improvement or change.

Here are some ideas for how to solve problems:

1. State what you perceive to be the problem.
2. Ask yourself, "What is the best long-term solution?"
3. Remember the results you are to produce.
4. Suspend all negative judgments regarding alternative solutions.
5. Replace all of your "but" words with "and" when brainstorming for solutions.
6. Put the problem into perspective ("Is it the worst problem I've had to face in my life?" "Exactly how time-consuming and costly is it to solve?" "Will it have irreversible consequences?")
7. Avoid "endless loop" questions (e.g., why, why, why . . .).
8. Ask empowering questions ("What might work here?" "Who might assist?" "What could be added or changed?").

What Is a Conflict?

The second common type of barrier is called a conflict. You have all had the unpleasant experience of dealing with conflicts at work, with your managers, your coworkers, and even with our customers. I have yet to meet someone who really likes conflict. Unfortunately, you cannot escape conflicts at work or anywhere else. There are, however, ways to resolve conflicts in a productive and professional way. But first we must define conflict.

Conflict is a struggle between opposing ideas, opinions, or beliefs. Conflicts always involve two or more people. Some typical conflicts that assistants experience on the job include the following:

- *Counterproductive moods.* You had a fight with your spouse this morning. When you arrive at work you are still angry, and you find it difficult to concentrate. Your manager wants a report completed in thirty minutes. How can you resolve this?
- *Lack of information.* Several months ago you were promoted above a coworker who has been at the company longer than you and who is several years older. Each time you approach him for information, he ignores you or somehow delays getting it to you. Your boss is expecting a report from you that requires figures that only this coworker can provide. You feel road-blocked. What actions do you take to resolve this conflict with your coworker?
- *Misuse of authority.* You support two managers. You have a meeting scheduled with Manager A at 8:30 A.M. to complete a project for Manager B by 9:30 A.M. But A doesn't show up until 9:00 A.M. and simply forgot your meeting at 8:30 A.M. It is impossible for you to finish the work in thirty minutes and deliver it to B by 9:30 A.M. What do you say to A to resolve the conflict?

Some of these conflicts may appear to be problems rather than conflicts; they could be both. The reason we typically don't want to deal with conflicts is that the situations have escalated from problems that were not solved or that received only a "band-aid" treatment, setting the stage for future conflict. The easiest way to distinguish between problems and conflicts is to remember that problems involve things (e.g., systems, situations, workflows, equipment) and need to be *solved*; conflicts involve people and are to be *resolved*. I have yet to hear someone say she has a conflict with the fax machine!

Consider this situation. Assistant A and Assistant B have shared workspace for six months (see Figure 6-2). Assistant A keeps her desk area very neat and organized. She always puts

Figure 6-2. Problem or Conflict?

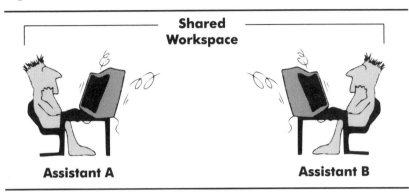

her pens and pencils in the drawer, makes sure all files are put away, and keeps her coffee cup clean after use. Assistant B, although not as neat and organized as Assistant A, does respect A's work style and does her best to remember to put things away. The actual workspace is small, making it difficult to keep things neat (according to B). Both are frustrated that there are not enough file drawers or desk space for them to work effectively. A is beginning to think that B is getting forgetful about keeping the workspace organized that she is deliberately making a mess. A mentions to B her observations about B's perceived sloppiness while B is working on an urgent project for her manager. B does not appreciate either A's approach or the pressure she is under, causing her to become irritated with Assistant A.

What do you think is the real problem in this situation? Which assistant perceives that there is a problem? How can she solve the problem, keeping in mind the long term? Is there a conflict between A and B? If so, what is it? Do you believe that a conflict created the problem? Do you believe that a problem escalated into a conflict? Do you think it is only a problem? only a conflict?

This scenario illustrates how complicated barriers can be and why it can be so difficult to solve or resolve them. The difficulty can be seen as a workspace problem that did not get solved by either A or B. B's lack of organization compounded the problem, which escalated into a conflict. Had either of them addressed the workspace issue immediately and explained her need for more file drawers and desk space, most likely the conflict would not have happened. Another way to look at it to suggest that neither A nor B saw the workspace as a problem because they were getting along fine until A noticed how unorganized B was. This continued to bother her, creating a conflict. Because of the conflict, the workspace suddenly seemed much smaller. If the assistants were to address their different work styles and resolve the conflict, the problem of workspace would no longer be an issue.

When you want to resolve a conflict with someone, make sure to pick a good time for *both* of you to discuss it. Just because you have an urgent need to resolve the conflict does not mean that the other person is ready. If you force the encounter, you will surely compound the conflict. In the workspace scenario, A did not think about her timing when she confronted B with her observations, as a result, she created a bigger conflict. Most of the time when we approach someone about a conflict, we want to prove that our view is right and we want them to understand our view; yet most of the time we are unwilling to hear the other side. When this happens, both people usually end up more frustrated and typically give up and don't ever really resolve the original conflict. Having one unresolved conflict between them makes it more likely they'll run into more conflicts and problems. Whenever you don't resolve a conflict, it leaves the door open to bigger ones in the future. Again using the workspace scenario, because A didn't use good judgment in deciding when to confront B, they will be looking for other things that don't work between them, and undoubtedly they will find them. This will make it even more difficult to resolve any future conflicts, because they will have to go back to the original conflict and resolve that one before they can move on.

Here are some guidelines and hints that can assist you in resolving conflicts more effectively:

1. Because it is important to state at the beginning what you want or hope to come out of the conversation, discuss your positive intention about the outcome you are seeking ("I want us to be productive and to be able to work without tension").

2. Describe your behavior in neutral terms, using "I" messages ("When [situation] happened, I felt [this way]. I need [this to happen] to feel better about this" or "When you gave me that report late, I felt angry and put on the spot. I need for us to come up with a solution so that this won't happen again.").

3. Acknowledge your part in creating the conflict. Be accountable ("I realize that I could have chosen a better time to talk with you when I knew you were really busy."). Apologize.

4. Let the person know you want to hear her view ("I would like to know your perception of what happened.").

5. Avoid interrupting or giving advice when the other person is speaking.

6. Let the person know that you are listening ("I understand you are angry.").

7. Make sure the timing of your discussion is mutually agreeable (set an actual time to get together and keep the appointment).

8. Let the other person know you will walk away if she becomes abusive (yells or uses language that is offensive). Tell her that it is impossible for you to resolve the conflict right now, and try to find another time to talk after emotions have calmed.

9. Follow through on the agreed-upon resolution (take the actions you committed yourself to and let the other person know that you have done so).

When you have a reactive or unproductive response to a barrier, you are viewing it as an obstacle destined to stop you in your tracks and to make you look bad in the eyes of others. Because you believe the myth that barriers are bad, you see them as reflecting negatively on your abilities and, therefore, as something that should not happen. Your reaction is to distance yourself any way you can—by hiding, by ignoring the situation, by blaming others, by panicking, or by digging in your heels and becoming immobilized.

There are several myths about barriers that lead people to

take unproductive stances in the face of a perceived obstacle. They include these fallacies:

- Barriers are negative.
- Barriers are permanent obstacles.
- Barriers should not exist.
- Barriers should be hidden.
- Barriers should be resolved alone.
- Barriers make you look bad.

Productive and Unproductive Responses to Barriers

No matter how good you are at your job, barriers will arise, and they certainly can keep you from creating results if you let them. Whether they keep you from producing your intended results depends almost entirely on you. Typically, when faced with any one of these barriers, people move into what is termed either unproductive behaviors and emotions or productive ones. These two stances are described in Figure 6-3.

Figure 6-3. Behavioral and Emotional Responses to Barriers.

Unproductive Behaviors and Emotions	Productive Behaviors and Emotions
Hiding	Acknowledgment
Ignoring	Assessment
Blaming	Action
Panicking	Reflection
Paralysis	Anticipation
Anger	Joy
Resentment	Pride
Resignation	Curiosity
Guilt	Satisfaction
Sense of Failure	Sense of Discovery

The Unproductive Stance

When you react unproductively when faced with a barrier, you aren't able to focus on your result, which jeopardizes your ability to satisfy your customer. This will most likely lead to more barriers.

Unproductive Behavioral Responses

1. *Hiding.* When you hide, you make a deal with yourself not to tell anyone else what happened. You try to "fix" the situation on your own, regardless of whether you have the skills and the information to do so. By the time you conclude that you can't fix it adequately, it is often too late to move past the barrier and reach a solution on time. By delaying, you are in danger of creating an even larger barrier than you already face.

2. *Ignoring.* When you ignore what you perceive as a barrier, you are simply putting your head in the sand, hoping that the barrier will disappear on its own or that somebody else will notice and take the right action. Ignoring the reality of a barrier means that, consciously or subconsciously, you are surprised that something came up to interfere with achieving your intended results. Then you blame the barrier for getting in your way.

3. *Blaming.* When you blame others for putting up barriers or blame the barrier itself, you are trying to put the responsibility on someone else. Blaming is the most used reactive behavior among employees. This reaction leads to countless other barriers (e.g., distrust, lack of respect, more miscommunication), which ultimately hurt job performance and keep you from being seen as a professional.

4. *Panicking.* When you respond with panic, you acknowledge that you are faced with a barrier but have little confidence that you can cope with it. Not stopping to examine exactly what happened, you make decisions and take actions that are often inappropriate or ineffective and that waste your time and others'. In this state of mind, you can become so overwhelmed that you start "steamrolling" others or simply get stuck.

5. *Becoming paralyzed*. Afraid that you simply cannot fix the situation or that to do so means having to change your behavior or your routine procedures, you back away or dig in your heels. You think the only action you can take is to cling fiercely to what you know.

You may know that these reactions are ineffective but feel powerless to respond differently. It takes years to develop a characteristic way of responding to what you perceive as negative events in your life. If you don't ever examine yourself, those reactions just take over and become comfortable. However, these reactions are more than nonproductive; they are disempowering, and they require a great deal of energy to maintain. In contrast, when you drop all those myths about "the way it's supposed to be" and stop blaming yourself and others when a breakdown occurs, everything becomes easier. You begin to turn your attention to inventing ways of solving problems and resolving conflicts. With practice over time, you begin actually to enjoy the process of resolving barriers.

The Productive Stance

Change your paradigm, and take another look at barriers. Knowing that as long as you take risks and learn new things, breakdowns will definitely happen, make the decision to shift your paradigm to a more productive way of dealing with barriers. It might seem difficult at first, but the rewards come soon.

When you take a productive stance (see Figure 6-4) toward breakdowns, you assume 100 percent responsibility for resolving them. In other words, you hold yourself accountable for what went right and what went wrong. Only by doing that can you start to look at barriers as opportunities.

Productive Behavioral Responses

1. *Acknowledging*. Recognizing and acknowledging the barrier facing you is a necessary first step. Surprisingly, once you are able to do that, ways of reaching solution begin to surface, and you can start moving forward.

Figure 6-4. The Productive Stance.

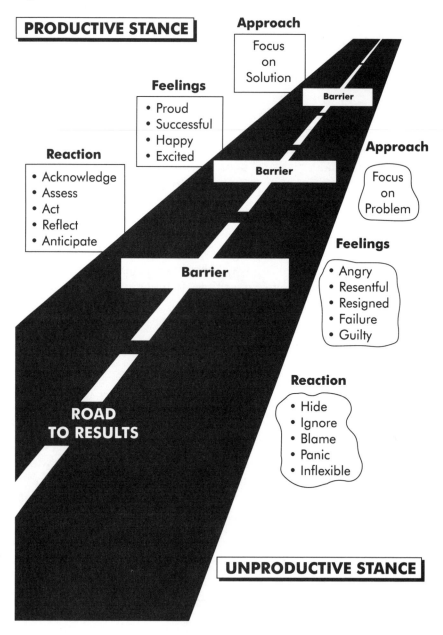

PRODUCTIVE STANCE

Approach
Focus on Solution

Feelings
- Proud
- Successful
- Happy
- Excited

Reaction
- Acknowledge
- Assess
- Act
- Reflect
- Anticipate

Barrier

Barrier

Barrier

Approach
Focus on Problem

Feelings
- Angry
- Resentful
- Resigned
- Failure
- Guilty

Reaction
- Hide
- Ignore
- Blame
- Panic
- Inflexible

ROAD TO RESULTS

UNPRODUCTIVE STANCE

2. *Assessing.* Once you admit that a barrier exists, you need to assess its importance. Does it really have the potential for sabotaging your results? Often, you find it does not, and you can disregard it. If it clearly can bring your project to a halt, then you can start to talk with others so that together you can create a solution.

3. *Acting.* Once you determine that the breakdown will cause havoc if left unattended, you can start to formulate a plan of action that allows you to move beyond it. Once you have created a plan and feel confident it will work, you then carry it out. Remember, this does not necessarily mean that you will be taking all of the actions. Look for others who can help when appropriate.

4. *Reflecting.* After you have resolved the situation and are back on track, it is important to reflect on what happened. If you don't take this step, the same problem can reoccur. When reflecting, it is useful to concentrate on describing the barrier clearly and fully. Think about how you might have contributed to it, and enlist the actions of coworkers to ensure that it doesn't repeat itself. Put your reflections in writing; you may want to redefine or update them later.

5. *Anticipating.* Ideally, you should make it a habit to anticipate things that might possibly get in your way. When you are in a position to anticipate a breakdown, you're in a better position to positively deal with it. This means you are constantly looking for whatever might get in the way of your ability to produce results.

Believing that barriers are opportunities will give you the necessary tools to achieve better results and recognition for handling barriers from a productive stance. Managers notice employees who are solution-minded. Remember to give yourself permission to make mistakes along the road to results. The key is to be accountable and to look at the mistake or barrier as an opportunity to learn, grow, change, and improve your productivity. Worksheet 4 offers you a chance to examine your ability to resolve a breakdown successfully.

Worksheet 4: **Resolving a Current Breakdown**

1. Name a breakdown or a possible breakdown you are facing at work.

   _____

   _____

2. What might get in the way of your producing the results you're committed to?_____

   _____

   _____

3. What actions can you and your coworkers take now to handle this breakdown?

   _____

   _____

4. If left unattended, will this breakdown stop you from creating results at work?_____

   _____

   _____

5. What new actions can you and your coworkers take right now to avert a future breakdown and create the results intended?_____

   _____

   _____

Summary

- Barriers are going to occur.
- Build time into your day for these interruptions.

- Anticipate and plan for breakdowns as often as possible.
- Remember that you always have a choice about the response or stance you can take—make it a productive one.
- When a breakdown occurs, ask yourself, Is this a problem or a conflict? Then take appropriate action.
- Remember that it is okay to make mistake. After all, it gives you an opportunity to learn.

Chapter 7

Getting On Track: Commitment to Results

To produce results that are valuable to your manager, team, department, and company, you must be committed to the end. *To commit yourself is to declare your intention to produce specific results and to do whatever it takes to create them.* When you commit yourself, it is critical that you honestly intend to do as you promise, not merely to try and hope for the best. Your focus is always on the overall result, not just on the actions or tasks you are taking to produce the result.

In your job, you constantly make commitments to your manager and to others for the purpose of getting work done and ultimately generating revenue for the companies. Your manager depends on the results you promise him. He uses them in his own work to create bigger results for his manager, who uses them to produce even bigger results, and so on. The sum of these results is the products or services the company provides to its customers. When you make commitments you don't intend to keep, you jeopardize your company's ability to meet its clients' needs. A company unable to satisfy its customers cannot be competitive and profitable over the long term.

Focusing on Results, Not Tasks

Often in work situations, you will find yourself working from a list of "things to do." You move down your list, checking off items as you complete them. When you work this way, you may get a lot of things done (like the busy bee), but they may not be top-priority items. This means that you have not routinely reassessed your "to do" list to make sure that what's on there is indeed necessary. If the individual actions you take don't directly contribute to moving you forward to produce your intended overall result, you are likely to waste valuable time and create problems for yourself and others over the long term. Being committed to getting your work done is different from being committed to specific results. The distinction is simple. You are not paid to work hard; you are paid to produce results.

To be truly successful at work, you are expected consistently to produce results that satisfy your manager. To do this, you need to know first what specific results your manager is responsible for producing. It is not enough to know what tasks you are responsible for producing, even if you know those tasks are supposed to support your manager's results. You must be committed to the results, not to the tasks, because you are ultimately accountable for producing them.

Take a moment and write down the top five results your manager or department are responsible for producing. If you are unable to do this, schedule a meeting with your manager to discuss this. You must be clear about the results your manager is committed to produce, for how can you possibly support those results if you don't know exactly what they are? Furthermore, your goals and objectives should directly support those results. If they do, when you achieve those goals, you are more likely to receive recognition and acknowledgment from your manager and your work team.

There are four steps you can take to practice committing yourself to the result.

Step 1: *Be Absolutely Clear About What the Specific Results Are Before Agreeing to Produce Them*

Your success in creating results depends on your knowing what specific "standards" will satisfy your manager and your customers. If the result is not clear from the beginning, it's more likely the outcome will not be what your customers want.

Complete the exercise in Worksheet 5 to put these concepts into action.

Worksheet 5: **Getting Clear About Results**

1. Name a project you have recently been asked to work on. _____

   _____

   _____

2. Who is this project ultimately for? Who is the customer? _____

   _____

   _____

3. What specific results are you to produce on this project? _____

   _____

   _____

4. What measures or standards will let you know that you have created the desired results? _____

   _____

   _____

5. Are you absolutely clear that these are the results you need to produce? _____

   _____

   _____

   a. If yes, how do you know? _____

      _____

      _____

   b. If no, what do you need to do to get clear? _____

      _____

      _____

Step 2: *Know What Resources Will Be Needed to Produce the Results Before Agreeing or Offering to Create Them*

Once the result is clear, think about the resources and competencies you will need to ensure a positive outcome. You need to know that these resources will be available to you; if they are not, this could stop the process of producing the results from the start. Take these actions to help you secure the proper resources:

1. Clarify the results before committing yourself to produce them. Understand what specific criteria they must meet to be successful. Consider this when making a decision whether to produce the result.
2. Assess who has the best skills to help produce the result.
3. Assess who is most available and can give the necessary time to produce the result in the time frame requested.

Complete Worksheet 6, which is designed to ensure the end result will be completed.

Worksheet 6: Securing Skills and Resources

For the same project you discussed in Worksheet 5, answer the following questions:

1. List the skills and resources needed to successfully create the results you've promised.

_____

_____

2. Are these skills and resources readily available?

_____

_____

   a. If not, what can you do to secure them?

   _____

   _____

Step 3: *Be Sincere About the Results You Intend to Produce*

Making a commitment is not synonymous with "trying." When you offer or agree to produce results for your manager, team, or company, you are giving your word. It is not that you will try to create them, or that you will do your best and hope that everything works out. When you say yes to a request, you are making a promise, and others will rely on you to keep that promise. As an assistant, giving and keeping your word is key to being seen as a valuable team player. Think about a time when you asked someone to do something and he said yes and then didn't deliver because other things were more important. How did that make you feel?

Work teams, departments, and organizations are networks of commitments made for the purpose of getting work done and ultimately producing results that will satisfy customers and produce revenue for the company. Most of the results produced are part of a larger goal. Sometimes your commitment may seem small. You may be standing at the copier to photocopy a fifty-page document for five people attending a manager's meeting. What would happen if your manager didn't receive the full fifty-page document, if the pages were out of order, or if there were not enough copies for everyone? How would this affect your reputation as a competent assistant? Would this create a breakdown or a potential conflict with your boss? You might say, "Well, it was a mistake" or "This doesn't happen very often," but this begs the question of your commitment to the result.

The commitments that you don't keep can jeopardize your company's ability to meet its customers' needs. A company that is unable to satisfy its clients cannot be successful and profitable over the long term. Try the exercise in Worksheet 7; it is designed to explore what happens when someone doesn't keep her commitment.

Worksheet 7: Committing Yourself to Create Results

1. Name the last time you were unable to create a result because a coworker did not keep a commitment to you._____

   _____

   _____

2. How did this make you feel? _____

   _____

   _____

3. How often does this happen to you? _____

   _____

   _____

4. What actions could you take to keep this from happening in the future? _____

   _____

   _____

Step 4: Take Whatever Actions Are Necessary to Produce the Intended Results

When you are truly committed to creating results, you are willing to take whatever actions are necessary to ensure that results meet the standards of the customer. This does not necessarily mean that you will take all the necessary actions yourself; it does mean that you will manage the process by which the proper actions are taken.

Managing the process of producing results requires that you continually evaluate whether the actions are moving the production forward. If they are not, then it is necessary to take steps to get things back on track as quickly as possible. The following steps are best taken as soon as you know what results are to be produced.

Planning

1. Decide what actions are to be taken and by whom.
2. Decide what specific resources (both human and material) will be needed.
3. Define roles and responsibilities when working with a team.
4. Develop a tracking system.

Requesting

1. Designate responsibilities when possible.
2. Recognize possible skill deficiencies, and request training.
3. Make requests for additional temporary help to meet a deadline.

Managing and Monitoring Progress

1. Check in frequently with customer.
2. Communicate with teammates regularly to ensure that they are keeping their commitments to the result.
3. Anticipate potential barriers, and resolve them before or as soon as they arise.
4. Report significant breakdowns to the manager or customer sooner rather than later.
5. Delegate the project to a peer (after confirming with the manager) when you are unable to complete it for some reason.

* * * * *

These four steps are key to making responsible commitments, ones that will ensure positive results. In the following case study, a worker doesn't follow the four key steps, and as a result all kinds of problems occur.

Steven promises his manager that he will have the financial report completed by Monday morning for Josephine's departmental meeting that afternoon. For Steven to keep his promise, he needs Carlos to give him the latest quarterly numbers from sales. Carlos needs to speak with the sales VP, Anna, to confirm the numbers before he gives them to Steven. Anna is out of town and won't be back until Monday afternoon, so Carlos holds off completing his report for Steven and doesn't bother to tell Steven about the situation. Monday morning arrives, and Steven's report is incomplete.

1. What happens when Josephine asks for the report?
2. What part does Steven play in the failure to produce the report on time for Josephine?
3. How will this failure affect their working relationship?
4. Who showed commitment, and how?

This is a typical scenario that happens all the time at work. If you are unable to keep a promise, it is your responsibility to inform your customer immediately and to renegotiate the request or offer a solution that allows the result to be achieved. The biggest complaint heard in offices around the country is people's inability to acknowledge early on that they will be unable to complete a task or produce a result. This behavior causes tremendous barriers and breakdowns within organizations and is the main reason that companies don't have their results completed on time. Take a moment and review these summary guidelines that will assist you in making responsible commitments.

Summary: Guidelines for Committing Yourself to Produce Results

- Create a plan for producing the result.
- Mobilize the necessary resources (human and material).
- Delegate specific actions to others, and monitor their progress.
- Ask for help as soon as you need it.
- Anticipate and resolve barriers.

Chapter 8

In With the New:
Adopting a Desire to Learn

Remember Sara from Chapter 1? She was eventually let go because of her inability to take on the new challenges and responsibilities presented to her. What if Sara had used the changes as an opportunity to learn? What if she had decided to put herself in a "learning mode" and actually looked forward to her new responsibilities? She would probably have kept her job, accommodating whatever new challenges came along and creating new ones to better her job. This Sara would be not only a change acceptor but someone with a desire to learn.

The fourth competency—adopting a desire to learn—is essential to achieving greater job satisfaction and recognition. This chapter focuses on the learning process at work, offering tips and exercises to help you gain a learning attitude to be successful in your role as a proactive work partner.

By its most general definition, learning is the overall process through which we acquire new knowledge. Most people associate knowledge with facts and information and consider themselves knowledgeable if they have gathered and stored a variety of facts, figures, and other information in their heads. I propose that knowledge is more than the memorization, storage, and application of information and facts. True knowledge is the ability to perform a particular action or activity and to have an understanding about that action or activity. This interpretation of knowledge does not discount the importance of information but sees information as a useful tool that helps people to learn new skills that will increase their capacity to create results for themselves or their managers, teams, departments, companies, and clients.

As a child, you probably asked a lot of questions, your mind constantly curious about the world you lived in. Only later in life did you become more guarded about your image and concerned about how you were perceived by others. Unfortunately, it is this fearful attitude that stops you from really moving forward in life. Why should you want to learn more? As illustrated in Figure 8-1, there are three basic reasons:

1. Learning is essential to innovation.
2. Learning helps you build confidence and competence.
3. Learning increases your value to yourself and to your company.

One of the primary keys to business success is creating new and improved products and services that satisfy clients. Continuous improvement (innovation) like this happens when you are in tune with your client's needs and are willing to constantly challenge what you produce and how you produce it for the purpose of finding a better way.

For businesses and other organizations, this requires that workers at every level be willing to redesign their work at a moment's notice in order to create results within their own jobs that contribute to overall customer satisfaction. Critical to this process is employees' willingness and desire to learn new skills

Figure 8-1. Why Learn?

Willingness to recognize needs and learn new skills is essential to innovation and to client satisfaction.

Helps you build competence and confidence.

Your value to yourself and to your company increases with each new skill you learn.

---

and ways of doing things for the good of themselves and their companies. Figure 8-2 illustrates the five stages of learning.

Stage 1: *Look*

The learning process is often initiated because you are personally interested in knowing an activity or because you or others see it as necessary for you to do your job or increase your contribution to yourself, your family, your team, your company, and your client. You have become aware that an activity exists and have decided that it is one you want or need to participate in. It is your interest or recognition of a need that generates your desire (choice) to learn the activity.

Stage 2: *Explore*

Once you've decided to learn a particular activity, you'll engage in a period of inquiry during which you'll learn the basic characteristics of the activity. Coming to know the characteristics of an activity familiarizes you with the resources, equipment, rules,

Figure 8-2. The Five Stages of Learning.

1. LOOK.	Look for skills or competencies that you want to learn. Understand the purpose or usefulness of the skill.
2. EXPLORE.	Ask questions, and become familiar with the characteristics of the activity. Learn about what it will take to learn this skill/competency.
3. ACT.	Create an action plan. Find a teacher or coach who can show you how to master this skill/competency. Schedule time. Take the necessary steps to learn the skill/competency.
4. REPEAT AND PRACTICE.	Repeat stages 1, 2, and 3, and practice, practice, practice until you have mastered the skill/competency. Ask for feedback from the teacher.
5. NOTICE.	Notice your progress, and acknowledge that you have gained a skill/competence through learning.

and actions you will utilize when performing the activity. Through reading, watching people who are competent in the activity, and asking lots of questions, you can learn about an activity by answering questions like these:

- What actions does the activity require?
- What resources and equipment will I use when performing the activity?
- What rules do I need to know to perform the activity effectively?

Stage 3: *Act*

In order to master a skill or competency, you need to take certain actions. But first, it is best to make a plan. People often forget to do this, mostly because they think it is obvious. When you skip this step, however, you may miss something important or delay your actual learning process. Once the plan is in place, take all the actions necessary to begin learning the new skill.

Stage 4: *Repeat and Practice*

In this stage, you continually repeat the steps or actions necessary to become capable of doing the activity on your own. It is helpful to have the guidance of someone who is competent in the activity to monitor your progress and to ensure that the steps you are taking are correct. Eventually the newly learned skill will become automatic after you have practiced it many times.

Stage 5: *Notice*

The last stage is to notice—notice the progress made, notice your mood or feelings about the learning process, notice what it's like to accomplish a goal, and notice what you've gained by learning this new skill or competency.

*   *   *   *   *

Practicing these stages of learning will make being a beginner a little easier. Although you may recognize the usefulness of learning, you may want to avoid it because of the pain and dis-comfort it can bring: When you learn, you move outside your comfort zone and expose your inefficiencies and incompetence, both to yourself and to others.

When you are engaged in the process of learning, if you listen closely, you can usually discern two voices speaking to you from within—your "player" and your "meddler." The player is the voice that recognizes the importance of learning and is excited to acquire a new skill or competence. The meddler is the voice in the background that has at least one hundred excuses why you don't need or should not learn the new skill.

Notice which statements are more familiar. We all have both voices, a negative one that can sabotage our efforts and a sup-portive voice that will keep us moving forward toward our goals. Each of us at any moment can choose which voice to listen to. So when you are uncertain about learning something new, just know it's the meddler getting in the way, and when you're excited, know it's the player encouraging the desire to learn. Review Figure 8-3, and decide which side has more influence over your learning process.

You also need to know that part of the learning process is

Figure 8-3. Meddler vs. Player Checklist.

Meddler	Player
How many barriers do you recognize?	*Do any of these sound familiar?*
❑ I'm afraid of failure/success.	❑ This will be fun!
❑ I just can't do it.	❑ I might get a pay increase.
❑ This is a waste of time.	❑ This will look good on my résumé.
❑ I can't see how this will help me.	❑ I can teach someone else.
❑ I'm too tired.	❑ I won't have to ask someone else.
❑ I really don't have the time.	❑ I feel more confident now.
❑ I don't want to look stupid.	❑ I can get a better/different job.

making mistakes. Mistakes are not a bad reflection on you as a person (that's the "meddler" talking). Mistakes are a natural part of learning, and they are to be expected. Learn to appreciate mistakes as opportunities to see where you can continue building competence in the new skill.

You may want to do the exercise in Worksheet 8. The learning process takes time. Each phase requires you to focus your attention and learn, step by step. When you are learning something new, you are considered a beginner, and most of us don't like to think of ourselves as beginners or novices, especially at work where we are already supposed to be competent in everything we do. This is the lie that no one talks about. It is impossible to innovate, improve, gain new knowledge, and, ultimately, learn if you already know it all. Besides, what fun is that? Being a beginner is a great place to be, because it means you are open to new possibilities for change, growth, and learning. Having a desire to learn is absolutely essential to enjoying greater job satisfaction.

There are several keys to successful learning. They include the following:

- *Acknowledge your incompetence openly.* It is okay not to know! This is the first step to learning.
- *Pay attention to your "player."* Your "player" is the voice within you that recognizes the importance of learning and is excited to forge ahead to acquire a new skill or competence.
- *Beware of your "meddler."* Your "meddler" is the voice within you that has at least one hundred reasons why you don't need to or should not learn a new skill. Don't let this voice stop you.
- *Give yourself permission to ask any question.* The only stupid question is the one you don't ask!
- *Give yourself permission to make mistakes.* Expecting perfection will only frustrate you.
- *Use mistakes and barriers as opportunities to see how you can continue to improve. Seek help when necessary.* Don't try to learn it all yourself. Find a mentor or coach you trust.

Worksheet 8: Learning a New Skill

1. Choose a skill or competency that you can learn to further your career and/or improve your job performance (e.g., time management, a new software program, project management, a database system). _____
2. Enroll in a class to learn the new skill or find a coach who is an expert and is willing to teach you.
3. Before you begin learning the skill, start a "learning journal." Write down the following:

   a. Your fears about learning the new skill _____

   _____

   _____

   b. Your excuses for not learning this skill _____

   _____

   _____

   c. How you will benefit from the skill once you've learned it ____

   _____

   _____

   d. How much time you will commit to learn this skill _____

   _____

   _____

   e. Your projected timeline for learning this skill _____

   _____

   _____

4. As you learn the skill, record your thoughts in your learning journal. Answer the following questions as you practice.

   a. What feelings are you experiencing while learning? _____

     _____

     _____

   b. How often does your meddler try to stop you from continuing to learn? What is your meddler telling you? _____

     _____

     _____

   c. How often does your player encourage your learning process? _____

     _____

     _____

5. After you have learned the skill, answer the following questions:

   a. How do you feel about yourself now that you've acquired this new skill? _____

     _____

     _____

   b. What other skills can you master that will help you in your job? _____

     _____

     _____

Summary: Guidelines for Learning

- When you learn new skills and competencies, you increase your own personal value to yourself and to your company.
- With the quick pace of change, what you know now may not be enough to create the kinds of results that are going to be wanted a year from now. What is important is not so much what you know but your ability and willingness to discover what you don't know and to take actions to learn it.
- What makes you valuable to your company is not how much you know right now but your ability to continue asking questions and learning more and more over time. This is really what you're paid for. If you do only what you know and wait for people to ask you to do things for them, you will limit your usefulness to your company.
- Be aware of your meddler.
- Pay close attention to your player.

Chapter 9

Bridging the Gap: Effective Communication

Did you know that miscommunication is the number one reason results aren't produced at work? Yet most people think of themselves as good communicators, and the truth is that most people are, *some of the time.* Being an effective communicator is not something you arrive at; it is a continual learning process. I have yet to meet someone who couldn't improve her communication skills.

This chapter focuses on how you can learn to be a better communicator. I explore the causes of miscommunications and the outcomes that happen when people miscommunicate; I also offer tips and tools for communicating more effectively. I look at both sides of communication: speaking and listening.

> *Communication is an ongoing process of sharing thoughts, feelings, ideas, and opinions through verbal and nonverbal behavior for the purpose of conveying a specific message to another person. When both the speaker and listener have the same understanding of the message, then the speaker has communicated effectively.*

Communication is complex because it involves people and their tone, language, experiences, cultures, personalities, and beliefs. Considering all this, it's no wonder we have miscommunications.

First and foremost, effective communication is dependent on your ability to be accountable. You must be willing to be responsible for what you say and how you say it. You are also responsible for the timing of conversations and how you listen in those conversations.

Figure 9-1 illustrates the different aspects of being an effective communicator. You are ultimately accountable for getting your work needs met, and it is through communication that this will or won't happen. The four aspects of communication in the middle of the diagram are critical to communicating effectively.

Timing

The first aspect of communication is *timing:* When you choose to speak or have a conversation, whether it is a meeting, a presentation, a request, or even a chat, it is critical that your timing be appropriate for the occasion. You need to be sensitive to the people with whom you are communicating. One of the most frequently heard complaints from managers is, "My assistant doesn't consider her timing." Remember Sue and her manager? Sue would run into her manager's office whenever he just got back from a meeting or business trip to ask him questions. Typically, he wasn't in his office for five minutes before she would barrage him with questions. He would get frustrated and angry because some of the questions were not that important and didn't need to be asked then. Sue, on the other hand, thought she was being proactive in her approach. She knew he wasn't in his office much, and she wanted to take advantage of the time that he was there so that she could proceed with her work. So both had legitimate complaints, but neither recognized that theirs was a simple problem that could be solved by having an

Figure 9-1. Communication Model.

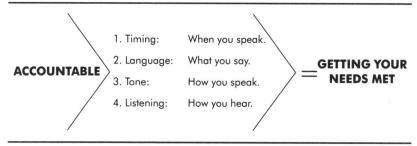

agreement about when it would be okay for Sue to ask questions. Once they were able to see this, they agreed that Sue would ask first, "Do you have time to answer several questions?" and then the manager would decide whether to answer those questions now or later.

Another important consideration is the amount of actual time needed for the meeting, presentation, questions, or request. You need to set up a time to meet, but you also need to allow the appropriate amount of time for the meeting. Support staff may schedule a meeting with their managers for an hour and wonder why it is disregarded. The assistant knows what she needs to talk about and she also knows that she and her manager sit down and meet fairly infrequently, so she wants to be sure she covers everything. This is a big mistake. Most managers don't have an hour at a time to give to their assistant. It is more effective to spend twenty minutes uninterrupted than forty-five minutes constantly interrupted and distracted.

It is also important to pause occasionally during conversations to give the other person time to reflect on what has been said and to ask questions. It's also considerate to be aware of your language so that you don't offend or insult the other person.

Language

The second aspect of communication is *language.* The words you choose, what you say, can disrupt the conversation or keep it flowing. Using words you know the other person doesn't like or that he considers "hot-button" words is irresponsible and unprofessional. Some support staff, for example, think the word *secretary* is offensive; for others, it is not an issue. Knowing that there are words that are triggers (two of my pet peeves are being referred to as a girl and being called cute), it is important that you be sensitive about the person to whom you are speaking, to be aware of people's "hot buttons" and not to push them in times of disagreement or conflict. Doing so will only create more problems and could potentially keep you from producing your results. Speaking clearly will bring you closer to getting your needs met (e.g., getting certain information) and minimize any potential breakdowns.

It is also critical to have an understanding about what you want to say before speaking. Usually, people do not take the time to get clear in their own minds the communication they want to deliver, whether in writing or verbally.

Tone

Tone—how you speak—is the third aspect of communication. How you speak is even more critical than what you say. Typically, when someone speaks in a sarcastic or condescending tone, people tune out on some level or become mad, resentful, or, in some cases, vengeful. It is your responsibility to let the other person, whether a coworker or a manager, know that that type of communication doesn't work.

Be aware of your tone when you approach someone. If you panic or are in a rush, you may use a begging tone or a demanding tone. Neither is useful for producing results. It is important that you maintain your dignity in all of your communications at work; using an inappropriate tone is the quickest way to lose it! Here is a short list of tones that are considered unprofessional:

- Whining
- Demanding
- Sarcastic
- Condescending
- Panicky or crisis-struck

Using any of these tones makes it very difficult for the other person to really hear what you have to say. And listening is key if you are to communicate effectively.

Listening

Listening, the fourth aspect of communication, is the skill people often forget about. Don't assume that because you have heard certain words the other person has said, you have listened. How many times has someone said he was listening to you, but his body language, facial expression, or lack of eye contact suggested that he really wasn't? And how many times have you done the same to someone else? If you aren't really listening, it will be impossible to fulfill the needs or produce the results you are paid for.

There are three levels of listening. The first is *listening,* or what I refer to as "pretending to listen." In this case, you hear the words and can recite them back, but they have no real meaning to you. The second is *active listening,* in which you ask questions to get a specific piece of information or other facts to do your job. You have an interest in what the other person is saying, so you are actively participating. The third is *listening for understanding.* In this case you take the time to make sure you know what the person is saying, look for any possible hidden meanings, and probe for continual understanding until you feel absolutely clear about what the person is trying to convey. Effective communication can happen only when the listener is listening for understanding.

Why is it so difficult to listen effectively? There are many distractions at work that can keep you from listening as best you can, including these:

- A wandering mind (pondering other things)
- Planning your response
- Interruptions (a ringing phone)
- Offers of unsolicited advice to the other person
- Tendency to finish the other person's sentence
- Physical functions (a hungry stomach)
- Greater interest in talking than in listening
- Wish to make the other person understand you
- Lack of interest in what the other person is saying

These distractions happen quite frequently, so it is important that you be willing to invest the necessary time and energy to ensure clear communication. (You can also try the exercise in Worksheet 9.)

You know what happens when people assume that communication is working. Some of the most common assumptions that stop people from communicating effectively are the following:

- Others know and understand what they are talking about
- If they "just listen," then they can understand the other person
- Everyone perceives the world the same way they do
- Other people attach the same meaning to words that they do
- Their communication was clear; the other person just wasn't really listening

Assumptions get people into all kinds of trouble, especially when they are trying to produce results. When you make these types of assumptions, you are no longer accountable for the consequences; you are leaving the outcome up to fate, hope, or anything else but yourself. This may work in your personal life, but it does not work in business. It is dangerous to make these or other kinds of assumptions at work. One simple assumption can snowball, creating a multitude of barriers that make it very difficult to repair whatever trust, respect, or confidence may have been damaged in the process.

Unless you learn to communicate well with your colleagues, it is very unlikely that you will be highly productive. Your company relies on you to be an effective communicator; after all, how else can you possibly get your work done? It makes sense, then, that the more effectively you communicate, the more likely it is that you will produce results that satisfy your customers, both inside and outside the company.

The technology of communication has changed rapidly over the past few years. We can communicate faster than ever before to places we never imagined. The fax machine, voice mail, electronic mail, and video conferencing have revolutionized our communication capabilities. With all of these changes, it is even more important to be clear in your communications. Wasted time spent on miscommunications is wasted dollars for the company. To produce specific results, you must communicate effectively. This happens when you are 100 percent accountable for both your speaking and your listening. Figures 9-2 and 9-3 ex-

Figure 9-2. Tips for Effective Speaking.

BE ACCOUNTABLE:	Accept total responsibility for your communication.
BE SPECIFIC:	Remember: who, what, why, when.
BE PREPARED:	Create an action plan; do your homework or research.
BE TIMELY:	Be sensitive to the timing and environmental "mood."
BE DIRECT:	State your desired result first, and add details later.
BE AWARE:	Know your communication strengths and weaknesses.

Figure 9-3. Tips for Effective Listening.

BE ACCOUNTABLE:	Accept responsibility for knowing and understanding what is asked of you.
ASK QUESTIONS:	Ask for clarity to ensure that you understand the purpose and result.
BE AWARE:	Be aware of the distractions that will affect your listening, and choose not to let them get in your way.
STAY FOCUSED:	Focus on the communicator and on what is being said. Catch yourself when you realize your mind is wandering.
BE HONEST:	Admit when you are not listening, and ask the speaker to repeat. If this isn't a good time to listen, let the speaker know, and set up a better time.
BE WILLING:	Accept the consequences when you don't listen for understanding. Listen better in the future.

plain how you can be ultimately accountable when you speak to and listen to each other. The exercises in Worksheet 9 will also help you to become a better listener.

By practicing these effective speaking and listening skills, you are ultimately practicing the Five Core Competencies. Effective communication encompasses the use of all of them.

Being an effective communicator is about continually being aware of your speaking and listening modes and the willingness to keep practicing the above tips.

Worksheet 9: **Learning to Listen Effectively**

The exercises in this section will help you become a better listener. The purpose is to focus on the speaker and what is being said, instead of giving in to distractions.

Part A

Over the next week, observe yourself in conversations you have with your manager and coworkers; then answer the following questions:

1. How often does your mind wander when you are in communication with others? _____

   _____

   _____

2. What effect does this have on your ability to produce results? ___

   _____

   _____

3. What are you willing to do to be a better listener? List actions. ___

   _____

   _____

Part B

If you noticed that your mind wandered frequently and you want to improve your listening skills, do the following exercise to help you stay focused in your communications with others:

As your manager or coworker is speaking to you, focus on her mouth for about thirty seconds (this sounds odd, but it works), not on her eyes, and silently repeat her words to yourself. This takes only a minute. You do not have to watch her mouth during the entire conversation. The purpose is to quickly refocus your mind on the conversation.

To benefit most from this exercise, I suggest that you practice it a minimum of three times a day for the next twenty-one days. Note how this affects your ability to communicate and produce results. Once you notice the improvement, share the exercise with your manager or coworker.

Now that you've had an opportunity to practice being a better listener, complete Worksheet 10, which assesses your ability to communicate effectively. It will show you how well you are currently communicating and what you need to pay attention to in your conversations with others.

Worksheet 10: **Evaluating Your Communication**

Review the list of communication characteristics on the left, and circle the number that you feel reflects your strength or weakness in that area. Strengths are defined as things you do automatically, without thinking, when you are communicating. Weaknesses are things you need to improve upon so that you can communicate more effectively. Note where you are strong and where you are weak. This is for your learning!

Strong   Weak

I. VISUAL

• Eye contact   5 4 3 2 1

• Facial Expression   5 4 3 2 1

• Body language   5 4 3 2 1

II. VOCAL

- Tone   5   4   3   2   1

- Timing   5   4   3   2   1

- Pauses   5   4   3   2   1

III. VERBAL

- Clarity   5   4   3   2   1

- Language   5   4   3   2   1

- Understanding   5   4   3   2   1

Once you've evaluated your ability to communicate effectively, remember to keep practicing. As we said in the beginning of this chapter, communication is an ongoing process. Your goal is not to be perfect; it's to improve your skills with every new situation. Your ability to speak clearly increases your productivity and improves your working relationships with your managers and coworkers. The more effective you are in your communication, the fewer barriers you will encounter and the less stress you will experience.

In the next chapter I introduce a model called the Productivity Cycle, which illustrates in much greater detail the connection between communication and results.

Effective Communication Checklist

❑ Know the purpose of the communications you engage in.
❑ Listen for what is *not* being said—read between the lines and respond appropriately.

(continues)

❑ Read body language.
❑ Articulate your specific needs clearly.
❑ Be *present* during communications—pay attention and don't let your mind wander.
❑ Ask questions when you are confused or unsure.
❑ Make sure those you communicate with are clear about what you have said.
❑ Speak up when you notice problems or have concerns.
❑ Make clear requests.
❑ Clarify requests made of you.

Part Three
The Productivity Cycle™

Chapter 10

Putting It All Together: The Productivity Cycle™

The better a company meets the specific needs of its customers and its potential customers, the more likely it is to be profitable and successful over the long term. Each of its employees has the responsibility to create results within their own jobs that support the company in achieving its mission of continual customer satisfaction.

With this as a framework, the key question is how to create results that consistently satisfy managers, teams, departments, executives, and clients. To explore the basic process by which results are created at work, we will start with a completed result and work backward to see how this result came into existence (see Figure 10-1).

Results are the consequences of the conversations that you have with others and the actions you take. Think about a result that was recently created for your manager. How did this result come about? Most likely, it came about because a number of *actions* were taken to produce it. Suppose, for example, that the result created for your manager was a weekly report on sales figures for the department's top salespeople. The completed report was placed on your manager's desk because specific actions were taken to produce it. Perhaps you interviewed each salesperson to find out his sales for the previous week. Then you compiled the figures into a report and formatted it on the computer. Then you asked a coworker to proofread your work. These are just a few of the actions taken. If you had not taken these actions, the

Figure 10-1. The Basic Results Model.

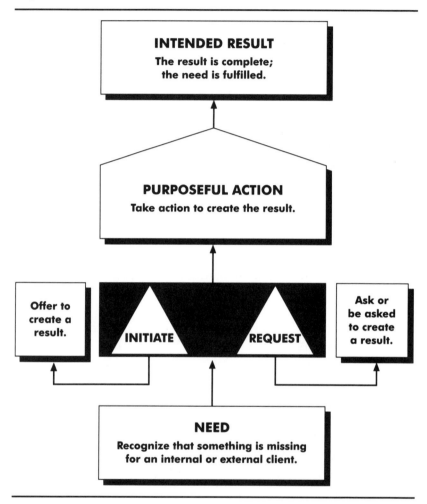

report would not exist and your manager would not be able to produce his results.

Now that you know that the report exists because you took certain actions to create it, the next question is, Why did you take these actions in the first place? Chances are that you generated this report because your manager *asked* you to. He made a *request*, either directly or indirectly, that you produce this report. Your actions were in direct response to this request.

Now you know that you took actions to produce the result because your manager asked you to. Why do you think your manager asked you to create this particular result for him? More likely than not, your manager had a specific *need* for this report to be produced in order to create another result for his manager or for a client. Almost always, results are produced within companies to fulfill specific needs. Employees work to fulfill the needs of those they work with and for. Together, their combined efforts fulfill the needs of the company's clients.

Your ability to produce intended results successfully within your company is directly related to the way you communicate with your clients, suppliers, and other workers. A company is nothing more than a network of communications through which people express their needs, ask others to do work for them, and agree to do work for others. These kinds of communications cause workers to take the actions necessary to create the results they need to satisfy customers, both inside and outside the company. The Basic Results Model is just the beginning of a much larger work flow process called the Productivity Cycle™. To ensure your job satisfaction and success within your job, it is your responsibility to have effective conversations (see Chapter 9) and take purposeful actions to produce results. You can choose to be a "results producer" by practicing the five Core Competencies and the Productivity Cycle (see Chapters 11, 12, and 13), which describes in more detail the process by which you can use the Core Competencies to create specific results.

The Productivity Cycle—The Team Perspective

As Figure 10-2 illustrates, the Productivity Cycle divides the work flow process into eight phases. Figure 10-2a emphasizes your role as a member of a team of people who, by communicating and working together effectively, are at the core of producing results.

The team includes more than just your manager or coworkers or departments. It also includes other administrative support staff regardless of what department they work in or who they support. It is critical that support staff band together and help

Figure 10-2. The Productivity Cycle™.

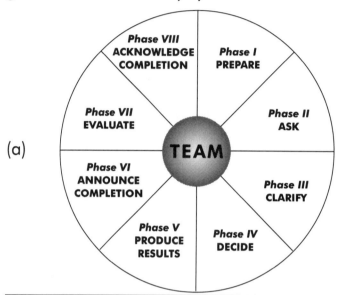

(a)

You are always part of a TEAM whenever you are producing a result.

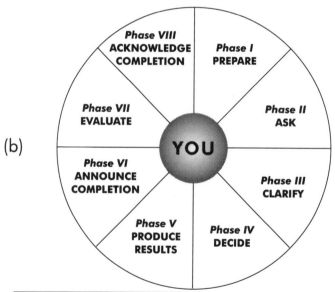

(b)

YOU are accountable for each phase of the work flow process
to ensure that the desired result is produced.

each other in their pursuit of greater job satisfaction and increased productivity.

Team building focuses on integrating individuals who both recognize their interdependence and understand that personal and team goals are best accomplished by mutual support. Members of a team feel a sense of ownership for their jobs and department because they are committed to goals they helped establish. Team members work in a climate of trust and are encouraged to communicate openly and honestly, as well as to express their ideas, opinions, and disagreements. They recognize conflict as a normal aspect of human interaction but view it as an opportunity to create a win-win situation by exploring different perspectives and frames of reference. Productivity is enhanced when team members participate in decisions that affect the group; this focuses everyone, including the leader, in the same direction. In addition, team members acknowledge each other for work well done. Review the objectives below and check those items that are practiced in the teams in which you participate.

Team-Building Checklist

❏ Determine the common goal.
❏ Is each person committed to support the team and each other?
❏ Does each member takes pride in any team success?
❏ Is communication open and honest?
❏ Is the expression of new ideas and suggestions about improved work methods encouraged?
❏ Are individuals recognized for personal contributions for the team?
❏ Do members receive support from the team to maintain balanced lifestyles?
❏ Are problems solved by the group as needed?

To summarize: A *team* is:

T   two or more people
E   equally committed to same results
A   actively supporting objectives
M   making results happen

Chapter 11

Making Clear Requests: Phases I, II, and III

Phase I: Preparing the Request

You produce results that will impact your work, the work of others, and the overall success of your company. It is important to prepare yourself to make requests that are specific, concise, and as clear as possible. By doing so, you make it more likely that your business needs will be met consistently. To prepare, you can brainstorm with yourself or with others to clarify what the final outcome should be. You can also refer to what I call an "Accountability Factor," which will remind you of your personal responsibility for preparing in advance to ensure that your results will be produced.

Accountability Factor #1

- **When making a request . . .** you are 100 percent responsible for preparing yourself to make a request that is as specific, concise, and clear as possible.
- **When receiving a request . . .** you are 100 percent responsible for helping those you work closely with to recognize their work needs and for encouraging them to make requests of you as necessary.

As the person preparing the request, you are 100 percent responsible for preparing yourself to make a request that is as specific, concise, and clear as possible. If you take the time to prepare, you will save time later as you eliminate miscommunication and lack of clarity. The person receiving the prepared request is responsible for assisting those you work with to recognize their work needs and for encouraging them to make specific requests of you to help them fulfill those needs when necessary and appropriate. Figure 11-1 illustrates this first phase of the Productivity Cycle.

When preparing requests, you need to take these steps:

1. Set specific results.
   • Think about what specific results need to be created to fulfill the need.
   • Know what specific requirements need to be met to show that the results have actually been created.
2. Create a realistic time frame for the results to be completed.
3. Determine the purpose for which you are creating these results.
4. Research who is the best person to help create the results. Ask the following questions:
   • Who is competent to produce the result?
   • Who has the time to produce the result?
   • Who has the time in her work schedule to help create the results? What is the difference?
5. What is the level of priority for this project?

It can be hard to see how you can play a role in preparing the requests that others make of you. How can you possibly be accountable for preparing a request if you are the person of whom the request is being asked? There are actions you can take and questions you can ask to prompt others to think of requests they need to make of you. When you do, you increase the chances that the requests will be made as soon as possible, giving you more time to produce the results expected. Here's an example.

An assistant can take responsibility for helping her manager prepare requests by scheduling daily agenda meetings with the manager. In these meetings, she can review with her manager the various meetings he attended and the phone calls he took

Figure 11-1. Phase I: Prepare the Request.

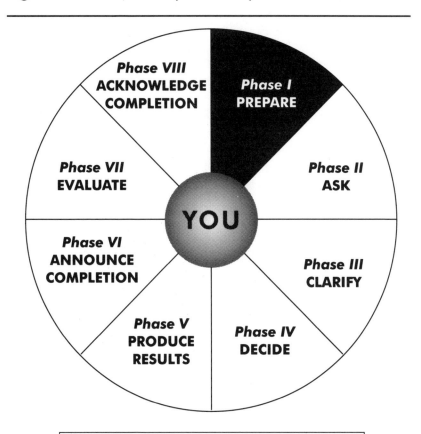

Ask yourself:
- **What is the desired result?**
- **Why do I need the result? (purpose)?**
- **When do I need the result? (time frame)?**
- **Whose help do I need?**
  - *—Who has the competence to help?*
  - *—Who has the time to help?*

during the day, and then she can ask questions he would not think of asking her [e.g., What do they talk about in these meetings?]. She can help him see what requests he could make of her or where she could make an offer to fulfill a need. She can also help him keep the promises he's made to others and track the promises that others have made to him.

Preparing a Request

When you aren't clear initially about the result you want someone to produce for you, you may get exactly what you asked for but not what you really wanted. This preparation phase is usually the one people don't take the time to do. I suggest you think of it as an investment in getting the results you want. If you take the time at the onset, you are more likely to be able to explain clearly to someone else what you want, increasing the probability that you will get it.

When I worked in Canada with a group of executive assistants, I phoned to ask for some soda to be brought into the room during a break. The woman on the other end of the phone asked me how much soda I wanted, and I said about twenty. She responded in a very shocked tone, asking if I was sure that I wanted that much soda. Fortunately for me, a participant standing nearby told me that I was asking for soda water and that what I wanted was pop or diet cola. If I had thought about where I was and what I was asking for *first*, I would have realized that in Canada soda means something different from what it does in California. I was lucky that one of the participants overheard; otherwise, I would have received twenty bottles of soda water. The point is clear: The simplest requests can be miscommunicated if not prepared first.

Suppose your manager is the vice president of sales and marketing for a large company. At the end of this week he will be attending an executive board meeting where he has been asked to give a presentation on sales for the coming year. As he's preparing his presentation, he realizes that he would like to give each board member a written report outlining last year's sales figures for comparison. Unfortunately, no report for last year's sales figures has been prepared. Because his schedule is extremely tight this week, he knows he will have no time to produce this report himself. He decides that he will ask you, on Wednesday, to write and produce the report for him. He knows that you just completed a large project and have the time, and he considers this project a priority over the others you are working on for him now. In other words, your manager has a need that he wants fulfilled.

Because your manager holds himself accountable (100 percent responsible) for the creation of this report (even though he will not actually create the report himself), he spends some time thinking about exactly what this report needs to look like and what specific content it must include before he actually makes the request of you. He decides that for the report to be useful in the meeting it must:

- Include a column of last year's sales figures by quarter for each of the company's five major product lines
- Include a column of the coming year's sales figures by quarter for each of the company's five major product lines
- Include a summary of total sales figures for both years
- Be ready in draft form for review by Thursday morning at 10:00 A.M.
- Be completed in its final form and copied (ten copies) by 5:00 P.M. Thursday
- Be made into a set of overhead transparencies by 9 A.M. Friday

Because of his preparation, you have a complete description of what is needed, which makes the job easier to produce.

Is there anything that you, as an assistant, could have done to get this request earlier? There is a way that would have encouraged the manager to think sooner about his needs, rather than wait until the last minute. Consider this scenario.

Two weeks ago, your manager asked you to put this particular board meeting on his calendar. At that time, you asked him what materials and resources he might need for the meeting. By asking this question, you sparked a train of thought that helped your manager recognize that he would need a sales figure report for last year. Once he recognized this need, you helped him create the result; alternatively, he could have asked you to create the result for him. This request was generated two weeks earlier because of your prompting.

Here are the four key questions to ask in preparing a request.

1. *Why?* Give the purpose for making the request. What is the bigger picture? How will fulfilling this need add value to your department or company?
2. *What?* State the specific result you want. What result, if produced, will fulfill your business need? By what specific criteria will the result be judged? What are the standards?
3. *When?* Include a specific time by which the result needs to be produced (e.g., Thursday, May 2, by 3:00 P.M.). Does this result take top priority? Is it possible to complete the result) by the deadline?
4. *Who?* Name the person most capable of producing the result. Who has the best skills and the necessary time to produce this result?

Using these criteria complete Worksheet 11, using a real request that you would like to make of your manager (e.g., asking for more regular meetings, soliciting a piece of equipment or software to make your job easier, asking for time off, seeking permission to attend a workshop). Then complete the exercise in Worksheet 12.

Worksheet 11: **Preparing a Request**

Think of a request that you need to make of your manager. Prepare the request using the following guidelines:

Why (purpose)? _____

_____

_____

When (time frame)? _____

_____

_____

Who (person)? _____

_____

_____

Action Plan: What do I need to do prior to asking? Is there information I need to gather before making the request? _____

_____

_____

Worksheet 12: **Prompting Others to Prepare Requests of You**

Schedule an agenda meeting with your manager (in person or by phone) every day for the next week. During these meetings, ask your manager to review the commitments he's made and the commitments others have made to him since you last met. Ask your manager what help he needs to fulfill his new commitments and to track those made to him. At the end of the week, answer the following questions:

1. How have the agenda meetings affected your working relationship with your manager? _____

   _____

   _____

   _____

2. What differences have you noticed in the timeliness of your manager's requests to you? Have there been fewer last-minute requests? _____

   _____

   _____

Phase II: Making the Request

In Phase II, the person who has prepared a request actually makes that request of someone she would like to create a result for her. Requests can be made in a number of different ways: verbally, in writing, over the computer, by voice mail. Accountability Factor #2 reminds you of the need to be clear in making requests.

   Accountability Factor #2

   - **When Making a Request . . .** *you* are 100 percent responsible for communicating your request as clearly as possible, whether speaking the request or writing it.

Figure 11-2. Phase II: Make the Request.

When you ask the person producing the result:
- **State the desired result.**
- **Provide a due date.**
- **State the purpose.**

- **When Receiving a Request ...** *you* are 100 percent responsible for paying close attention when listening to or when reading a written request. Listen for clarity.

It is crucial at this stage that both parties communicate effectively while the request is being established. It is the requester's responsibility to make sure that the requestee has a clear understanding of what is being asked of her. If the requester assumes because the requestee says yes that everything is fine, the requester is not being accountable for the completion of the request. At the same time the requestee is also equally responsible for asking all necessary questions so that she is absolutely clear about what needs to be produced. She will be held accountable for the actual production of the results, so it is her responsibility to know what is being asked of her.

When you make a request, you are 100 percent responsible for communicating the request as clearly and concisely as possible. Clear requests should give the listener the following information:

- Results to be created
  —Specific requirements to be met
  —Standards by which results will be measured
- Reason for creating results
- Time by which results must be created

When you receive a request, you are 100 percent responsible for paying careful attention when listening to or reading the request. Here are some tips to help you listen better:

- Take notes if necessary.
- Listen closely for the basic information you need to fully understand the request.
- Know what overall result is to be created.
- Know what specific requirements are to be met.
- Know the time by which the result must be created.
- Know the purpose for creating the result.
- Ask for the request in writing if necessary.
- Ask yourself, "Am I clear about what is being asked of me?"

By being as clear as possible in Phase II of the Productivity Cycle, you reduce the time it will take to clarify the request and get into action. When you don't communicate a request clearly to begin with, you have to spend time later explaining and clarifying it before others can move on to fulfill it. This is a waste of valuable time that can easily be avoided. Complete the exercise in Worksheet 13 to practice making clear and specific requests.

Worksheet 13: Requests: Yours and Those of Others

Your Requests:

Make the requests you prepared for, considering all the criteria you have learned so far: _____

_____

_____

_____

_____

Others' Requests:

Record your observation of others as they make requests. Could the requests have been clearer? Do they meet the standards we have described? _____

_____

_____

_____

_____

Phase III: Clarifying the Request

After a request has been made and before any action is taken, the person making the request and the person receiving the request must confirm that they have a common understanding of

Figure 11-3. Phase III: Clarify the Request.

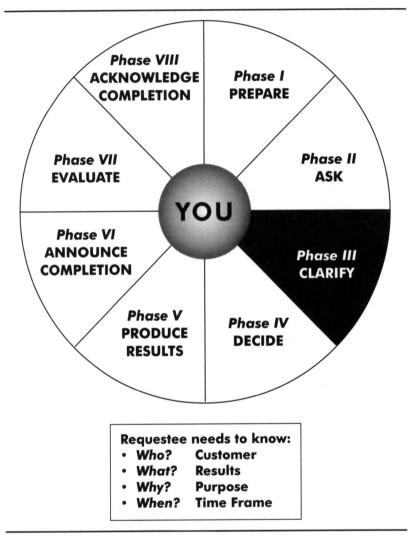

Requestee needs to know:
* **Who?** Customer
* **What?** Results
* **Why?** Purpose
* **When?** Time Frame

the results to be produced (see Figure 8-3). Consider also Accountability Factor #3.

Accountability Factor #3

* **When Making a Request** . . . you are 100 percent responsible for ensuring that the person of whom you make the

request is clear about what specific result you want produced.

- **When Receiving a Request . . .** you are 100 percent responsible for asking whatever questions are necessary to understand what specific result you are being asked to produce.

Both the requester and the requestee must understand these points:

- *Who the customer is.* Anytime you create results, you create them for someone, for a reason. The person you create the result for is your customer. Usually the customer is the person who made the request, but it can be someone other than the requester—your manager, your manager's boss, a coworker, or even your client. You can have more than one customer, and customers can be internal or external.

The customer is the person you have to satisfy. If at any time during the process of creating results you have questions, concerns, or problems, your customer is one person to consult.

- *What the desired results are, and by when.* Before you commit to produce results for a customer, you need to be absolutely clear about what you are committing to create. You must make sure that you know what specific requirements you are to meet, and by when. (Requirements are the specific criteria that need to be present in the final result in order for the customer to be satisfied.)

If you begin taking action to create results before you are sure you understand the results your customer wants, you run the risk of producing results that do not satisfy the customer. When this happens, it will be necessary for you to recreate the intended results, a use of additional time, resources, and energy that could have been avoided had you been clear about what was wanted from the beginning.

- *Why the results need to be created.* All results are created for a purpose. When you are producing results for others, it is extremely useful to understand what greater purpose these results will be used for. When others ask you to produce a result for them, often they need to use this result to produce another result for their manager or to prepare for an important conversation with their manager. If you understand the purpose of the result, you can help the other person create similar results that can be used to meet a similar need at a later date. This is anticipating needs on the basis of similar past experiences—in other words, being proactive.

During Phase III, as the person clarifying the request, you are 100 percent responsible for ensuring that the person of whom you are making the request is clear about exactly what results are expected. To ensure that this will happen, you can:

- Ask if there are any questions.
- Ask the person to tell you what she thinks you expect.
- Make sure that what she says is indeed what you expect. If it is not, give her whatever details she needs to get clear.
- Recheck her clarity before she begins to create the results you want.
- Ask if she has any suggestions.

By explaining why you want her to produce the results, you give her the opportunity to make suggestions about how the results can be enhanced and to contribute to the result, which enhances her ownership of the outcome.

When you receive requests, you are 100 percent responsible for making sure you understand exactly what results you are expected to produce. You must make sure you know:

- *Who* your customer is
- *What* specific results you need to create
- *Why* you are creating the results
- *When* you need to create the results

Here are some other tips to help ensure that the desired result is complete:

- Ask questions when you are not clear.
- Tell the person who made the request what specific results you think she expects you to create for her.

Worksheet 14: **Getting Clear About Results**

1. Name a new project you have recently been asked to work on.

   _____

   _____

2. Whom are you working on this project for? (In other words, who is your customer for this project?) _____

   _____

   _____

3. What specific results are you expected to produce for your customer on this project? _____

   _____

   _____

4. How will you know when you have created these results? (What specific criteria do you need to meet?) _____

   _____

   _____

5. Are you absolutely clear that these are the results you need to create?

   a. If yes, how do you know? _____

   _____

   _____

   b. If no, what do you need to do to get clear? Take action! _____

   _____

   _____

- Ask her to confirm that these are the results she wants.
- Offer ideas for additional or alternative results that could help serve the same purpose as this result.

Complete exercise in Worksheet 14 to help you clarify the results that currently need to be produced.

Chapter 12

Making Purposeful Decisions and Achieving Goals: Phases IV and V

Phase IV: Making Decisions

Whenever someone makes a request of you, you must decide whether you will create the results the person wants. You have three basic options to choose from: You can say *yes*, you can say *no*, or you can *negotiate*. Before making a choice, consider Accountability Factor #4.

Accountability Factor #4

- **When Making a Request . . .** *you* are 100 percent responsible for making sure the requestee makes a responsible decision. Be confident that she has the competence and the time to fulfill your request.
- **When Receiving a Request . . .** *you* are 100 percent responsible for making a responsible decision about whether you can produce the intended result.

To help you make your decision, you should consider these factors:

- Do you have the skills you need to produce the results? If not, can you learn them quickly enough to create the result in the required time frame?

Figure 12-1. Phase IV: Decide.

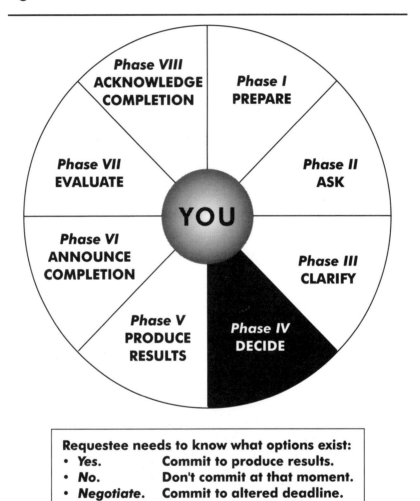

Requestee needs to know what options exist:
- **Yes.**   Commit to produce results.
- **No.**   Don't commit at that moment.
- **Negotiate.**   Commit to altered deadline.

- Do you have the time to create the result, given the other results you have committed to produce? If not, is it possible to reprioritize your work so that you can free up the time to create this result and still produce the others?
- Are the various actions you think you will need to take consistent with your own personal standards, boundaries,

and values? Are you willing and able to take all the actions necessary to produce the result you are agreeing to?

Suppose your manager asks you to make travel arrangements for him. It is not business travel, however; he wants to go fishing with two buddies. This is going to take up more time than you want to spend. What do you do?

Saying Yes

When you say yes, you are giving your word, promising to create the results the other person wants produced. Saying yes, then, indicates your intention to take whatever actions are necessary to create the result. You are confident that you can mobilize the resources and talents, both yours and others', to create the results. This means that you will see to it that the result is produced when it is required.

Saying No

When you say no, you are not committing to create the results asked of you. This does not mean that you say no and simply walk away. Saying no is about exercising the option to say no under certain agreed-upon conditions. You need to know that you can say no when it is appropriate. The best way to do this is to make an agreement with your manager about when it is okay to say no. It is critical that you get this agreement up front before you exercise the option of saying no.

Saying no also does not guarantee that you will not produce the result; it is an opportunity to have a conversation about your workload and your priorities. In this conversation, you can inform your manager about what is on your "to do" list and the various projects you are currently working on. The purpose of saying no is to let your manager know that you are unable to produce the result *at that time*. After discussing the various circumstances, you may change your decision, or perhaps someone else is in fact better able to produce the result.

Reasons We Say No	*Reasons We Don't Say No*
• We lack time.	• We fear looking incompetent.
• We are overwhelmed.	• We want to look good.
• We are acting accountably.	• We fear being labeled a "non-
• We don't have skills.	team player."
• We lack the necessary re-	• We fear losing our jobs.
sources.	
• We are unclear about our priori-	
ties.	
• We have family/personal obli-	
gations.	

Complete Worksheet 15 to practice choosing an appropriate response to a request for a result. Then consider this example of why it is important to say no when you know you are unable to produce the result at that time.

Suppose your manager has asked you to train the administrative support staff in the new branches of the company throughout the United States. Producing this result would require that you travel to other states for three weeks out of every month for the next year. You have two young children and have made a personal commitment to be home three nights a week to spend time with them. Accepting this request would not allow you to keep this commitment. How do you approach your manager? If you have an agreement about saying no, this request will be much easier to discuss; if you don't, it will be trickier, because your understanding of your needs and rights may conflict with your manager's ideas about your responsibility to the company.

You may believe that it is impossible to say no in your job. You may think that if you say no, you will be seen negatively by those you work with and that you may even lose your job. The opposite is true. Managers would rather know the truth about whether the result can really be produced. When you say yes instead of what you need to say—no—then you may not produce the results that you promised. This is much riskier than saying no.

Worksheet 15: **Making a Responsible Decision**

What is the request?_____

What is the desired result? _____

Assess the following:

✍ **Skills required** _____

✍ **Time needed** _____

✍ **Help needed (people/resources)** _____

If You. . .	Recommended Response
Have the skills, time, and help required . . .	Say yes
Have the skills and help but don't have the time . . .	Negotiate (ask for more time)
Have the skills and time but don't have the necessary help . . .	Negotiate (ask for more resources/help)
Have the time but don't have the skills and help . . .	Say no with explanation (offer solution/ask for training)
Don't have the skills, time, or help . . .	Say no with explanation (offer solution)

Saying no is often in the best interest of the results in question. If you know you are unable to produce them or that you don't have the time, the responsible decision is to say no. By saying no, you allow the person who needs the results to move on and find someone who can create them.

How your no is viewed by others depends on how you say it. There are two ways of saying no: plain no and a justified no. When you say a plain no, you decline to create the desired results but do not offer any reason. This is not recommended; it can seem defiant and often puts others on the defensive. If you say no often enough, you probably will not have your job for very long.

When you say no, it is useful to offer some sort of explanation. This kind of no appears responsible and cooperative and can help determine who might be able to create the results. When you say no, offer alternatives to the person who is making the request of you. Help him to think of other coworkers who may be able to create the results or of other ways to create the results.

Suppose your manager asks you to proofread a very detailed fifty-page financial document by the end of the day. You are currently working on three other projects that also have to be completed by the end of the day, and you know that you do not have enough time to do the proofreading by the time your manager needs it. You tell him you cannot proofread the financial document because you are working on three other projects. By saying no this way, you help your manager understand why you are not able to create the result. He can then ask if you know anybody else who could proofread the report or who could help you with the other projects so that you could proofread the report.

It is important to exercise the right to say no when it is necessary. If you don't, you jeopardize the results being produced and, potentially, your self-respect and the trust of others. As previously mentioned, when you say yes, you are giving your word, so each time you say yes when you really want to say no, you go against what you know to be best. Soon saying yes won't mean anything, and eventually you will lose your credibility and self-respect. You may also reduce the trust between you and your manager.

Exercising the right to say no allows you to open up a dialogue with your manager and to work as a team at restructuring and reprioritizing projects. This process increases productivity and enhances your work relationships.

These tips for saying no may be helpful to you:

- Explain why you cannot create the result at that time.
- Offer a legitimate reason (i.e., lack of skill or time).

- Check and readjust priorities if necessary.
- Offer an alternative solution.
- Suggest another person or another way to produce the result.

Negotiating

The last and most important option is negotiation. Negotiating is a skill that takes continuous practice if you are really to excel at it.

Negotiation is part of your daily communication with your manager and your coworkers. The better your are at negotiating, the more likely you are to have your work needs met, be less stressed, and have more job satisfaction.

Negotiation requires using the five Core Competencies in all of your communications. Whether you are seeking more time for a project, more resources, or more pay, you need to know how to be a successful negotiator.

The exercises in Worksheet 16 on the next page allow you to practice the three possible responses to requests. Complete these exercises before moving on to Phase V.

Worksheet 16: Making Decisions

1. Think of a recent request to which you said yes. Was it appropriate to say yes? Were you sure that you would be able to produce the result? Describe. _____

   _____

   _____

2. Think of a recent request to which you said yes when you wanted to say no. How did your decision affect your ability to produce the results that you committed yourself to? What could have changed if you had said no? Describe. _____

   _____

   _____

3. Think of a recent request when you used your negotiation skills. How did negotiating help you produce the result? Describe. ____

   _____

   _____

4. Make a request. _____

   _____

   _____

Phase V: Producing the Results

After you make a responsible decision and have committed to producing the result, you must actually create the promised result. Do the exercises in Worksheet 17 on page 152. Refer to Accountability Factor #5 before reading further.

Figure 12-2. Phase V: Produce the Results.

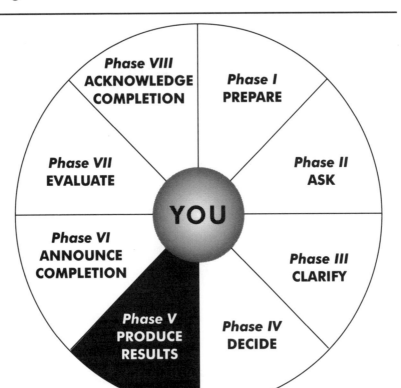

A winning approach:
- **Create a plan.**
- **Take action.**
- **Look for and resolve barriers.**
- **Keep the customer informed of progress.**

Accountability Factor #5

- **When Making a Request . . .** *you* are 100 percent responsible for making sure that progress toward creating the result is on schedule at all times.
- **When Receiving a Request . . .** *you* are 100 percent responsible for taking whatever actions are necessary to create the result your customer expects.

Worksheet 17: Planning to Produce a Result

Think of a result you recently promised to create for your manager. Answer these questions to help you plan how you will produce this result.

1. What specific actions will I need to take to produce the result?

   _____

   _____

2. When must each of these actions be taken? _____

   _____

   _____

3. What resources (materials, equipment) will I need to create the result? How will I secure these resources? By when? _____

   _____

   _____

4. Whose help do I need? When will I request the help? _____

   _____

   _____

5. What barriers could stop me from creating the result my customer wants? What actions can I take now to keep these problems from happening? _____

_____

_____

6. How often will I assess my progress toward creating the result? When? _____

_____

_____

7. How often will I inform my customer of my progress? When?

_____

_____

The person producing a request is 100 percent responsible for making sure that the result will be produced on time. The person receiving a request must be committed to producing the result and to taking whatever actions are necessary to satisfy the customer. During Phase V, it is critical that you take the following steps:

1. *Planning.* Before you begin taking action to create a result, it is helpful to develop a blueprint of how you will create the results. Using Worksheet 18 may guide your progress. Your plan should outline the various actions you will take, with due dates, in order to create the result your customer wants. It is important to brainstorm when developing your plan; sometimes others see actions you can take to create results that you may not see ourselves.

Your plan can and most likely will change as you progress. Part of the planning process is constantly evaluating whether the actions you are taking are effective in moving you toward completing the request. As barriers arise or as you notice that

Worksheet 18: **Planning for Producing Results**

Project:			Due Date:	
Desired Result: _____				
Criteria for Completion: _____				
Who	**Action Plan**	**Potential Barriers**	**Progress Report to Customer**	**Date Completed**

your actions are ineffective, you may find it necessary to revise your plan, taking the new factors into consideration.

When developing your plan for creating results, ask yourself the following questions:

- What "mini"-results do I need to produce in order to create the overall result my customer expects? By when?
- What specific actions will I and/or others need to take to produce these mini-results? By when?
- What resources will I need to create these results?
- Whose help will I need?
- What requests can I make of others? By when?

2. *Taking action.* Once you have formulated your plan, you can begin taking the actions necessary to create the results you have promised your customers. Keep reassessing your actions and try to anticipate any potential barriers.

3. *Anticipating and resolving barriers*. Throughout the process of creating results, you must constantly be on the lookout for barriers that could keep you from creating your result. If you see a potential barrier, begin to take actions to stop it from arising. Here are some questions to ask yourself as you try to anticipate barriers:

- What barriers could possibly get in the way of my creating the result my customer wants?
- What actions can I take now to keep these barriers from arising?

When unforeseen barriers do present themselves, do not let them stop you from creating results for your customers. You can respond productively and creatively to these barriers by:

- Recognizing and acknowledging the barrier
- Assessing whether the barrier has the potential to stop you from creating your result
- Planning and taking action to eliminate the barrier

4. *Reporting progress to your customer*. It is imperative that you let your customer know your progress in producing the result. You should also report on any barriers that could slow you down or stop you from creating the result in the time frame you agreed to.

Checking in with your customer gives him the opportunity to ask questions or to make changes to the result being produced. Customers would rather know sooner than later if there is a snag.

Chapter 13

Completing and Implementing Decisions: Phases VI, VII, and VIII

Phase VI: Announcing Completion

After you have produced the result desired by your customer, it is important that you let the customer know that the result is complete and ready for his review. Unless you let your customer know you are finished, he may be left wondering. You can put his mind at ease by letting him know you are done. Also consider Accountability Factor #5 and Figure 13-1.

Accountability Factor #6

- **When Making a Request . . .** *you* are 100 percent responsible for asking for the completed result if you have not received it by the due date.
- **When Receiving a Request . . .** *you* are 100 percent responsible for letting your customer know that the result is complete.

The person who made the request is responsible for checking to see if the result is complete when it is expected to be. When you are finished creating the result for your manager or

Figure 13-1. Phase VI: Announce Completion.

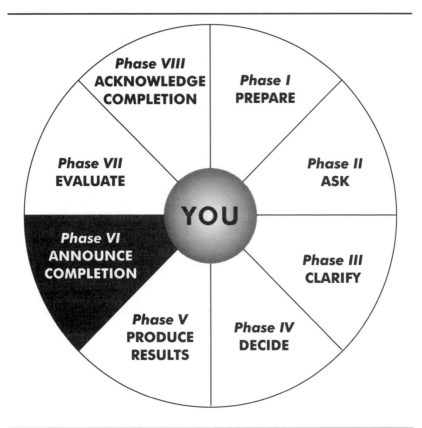

Let your customer know that you have produced the results.

a coworker, you must let him know you have completed your work.

Phase VII: Evaluating Results

The process of creating intended results is not complete until the customer expresses satisfaction with the result produced. This is important, since the customer will use the result to produce other results within his work. Accountability Factor #7 is a reminder of your primary responsibility.

Accountability Factor #7

- **When Making a Request** . . . *you* are 100 percent responsible for reviewing completed results to assess whether the standards you requested were met.
- **When Receiving a Request** . . . *you* are 100 percent responsible for making sure your customer reviews the results you created to assess satisfaction.

As the customer, before you can express satisfaction, you must evaluate the result (see Figure 13-2). Your job as the evaluator is to make sure the specific results that were requested have been achieved. As the customer, you are 100 percent responsible for reviewing the completed results to assess whether the requirements you laid out have been met. If they have, you can move on to Phase VIII and thank the person who created the result for you. If they have not, you must determine what is missing and request the person who is creating the result take new actions to fulfill it, complete the task. First, however, you should do the following:

- Reclarify the request (Phase III).
- Be specific about the result.
- Set a new due date that is agreeable to both parties.

As the producer of the results, you are 100 percent responsible for making sure that your customer reviews the results you created and assesses their acceptability. If the customer is satisfied, you need to ask for feedback. If he is not satisfied, then you must do the following:

- Reclarify the request (Phase III).
- Make a new decision (Phase IV).
- Take appropriate actions (Phase V).
- Announce completion (Phase VI).

The next time someone produces a result for you, use Worksheet 17 to ensure that all the criteria were met.

Figure 13-2. Phase VII: Evaluate Completion.

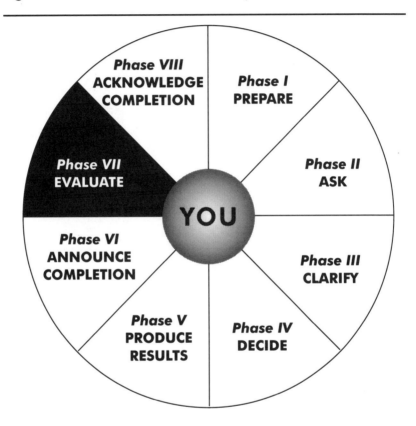

Customer asks, "Was the desired result produced?"
- **If *yes*, move to Phase VIII.**
- **If *no*, go back and repeat Phases III–VI.**
  —Reclarify desired result.

Worksheet 19: **Evaluating Results.**

Date Received	Date Due	Date Completed	Desired result	Evaluation	Completion acknowledged

Phase VIII: Acknowledging Completion

Productive work deserves acknowledgment. It is up to you to see that you receive it. Accountability Factor #8 reminds you how to do this.

Accountability Factor #8

- **When Making a Request** . . . *you* are 100 percent responsible for thanking the requestee for producing the result.
- **When Receiving a Request** . . . *you* are 100 percent responsible for making sure your customer is satisfied with the end result. Acknowledge yourself for work well done.

Phase VIII completes the process of producing a result. Without this phase there is no closure and we all need that to move on to the next project, task, assignment etc.

As a customer, you must thank those who produce results that satisfy you (see Figure 13-3). By doing so, you empower and motivate them to continue producing quality work. It doesn't

Figure 13-3. Phase VIII: Acknowledge Completion.

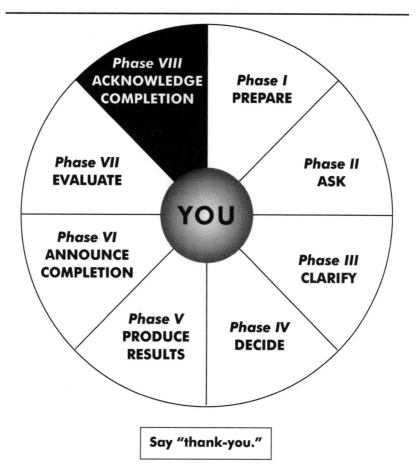

Say "thank-you."

take much time or effort to acknowledge someone's contribution, no matter what your job title, and you know how great it feels when you are praised for good work, especially if it is something that took a long time to complete.

If you are not getting the acknowledgment you deserve, then it is up to you to ask for feedback about your performance. Usually when you don't hear from your customer after you've presented him with a result he requested, you assume that he is satisfied. While this may be true, you need to make sure that he has reviewed the result and determined that you met all his requirements. Until you do this, you cannot consider the project complete.

If your customer has not acknowledged his satisfaction with the result, you should check with him to make sure that he is pleased. Don't wait for review time. Ask along the way: "Was that report I gave you satisfactory?" or "Did the project meet your expectations?"

In coaching managers, I have found that most managers simply forget to say thank you, not because they didn't want to say it but because they were too busy doing what they needed to do to produce their results. That is why it is even more important to ask for feedback; it serves as a reminder to them that they are not giving acknowledgment or completing the work flow process.

When you have created a result for your manager or for a coworker, you are 100 percent accountable for making sure that he is satisfied with the end product. When it is completed the customer is satisfied, you too must acknowledge yourself for work well done. This completes the work flow process.

The importance of the Productivity Cycle is to make you more effective in your communication in order to produce results consistently. The more people are familiar with the Productivity Cycle, the more effective they will be in their work flow process.

In conclusion, The Productivity Cycle serves as a tool to ensure consistent quality results that satisfy the customer and increase our own value to the organization—as well as our job satisfaction.

Part Four
Conclusion

Chapter 14

A Bridge Complete:
Some Final Thoughts

Some final thoughts about the importance of administrative support staff leading the way into the twenty-first century. The simple truth is that it is up to each and every one of you to take a risk with your managers, coworkers, and most of all, yourselves if you are to change the old paradigm perception of support staff. This means that it is up to you to help your managers, coworkers, and organizations to see your value by your positive attitude and your purposeful actions. As the new middle management, you are responsible for shifting the paradigm, asking for what you need and want in your jobs and work relationships; by changing that paradigm you will contribute to your companies' competitive edge in the global marketplace and help increase overall productivity. The change may not be easy or quick. More likely it will take time, patience, and perseverance, but I believe it is worth it.

Many of your work relationships suffer from a lack of clear communication, active teamwork, and well-defined expectations and goals. However, you now have new skills and tools that will help you begin to change. You have the opportunity to influence employee morale and the organization's bottom line with your words and your actions. The Five Core Competencies and the Productivity Cycle will guide you in your efforts to be recognized, acknowledged, and paid for your expanded and critical role and will help put you in a position to form the business partnerships you need to remain globally competitive and professionally successful.

As I mentioned in the beginning of this book, Ellen Bravo of Nine to Five describes two distinct options open to you—to start valuing yourselves or to wait for management and the business world to call the shots. You need to stand up for yourselves to create the possibilities and the positive changes in the workplace that bring the rewards of greater job satisfaction and more recognition. You need to ask your managers and your human resources personnel for more and better training focusing on the managerial, interpersonal, and team-building skills you need to be successful in your role.

You need to remember that you do have enormous influence on organizational productivity and customer satisfaction. If you don't function well with your managers, coworkers, or customers, the effect on the organization could be devastating. It is time that support staff acknowledge themselves for their tremendous contribution, especially in today's changing business environment of downsizing, reorganizing, restructuring, and technological advances. Are you going to continue to allow others to disempower, disrespect, and underpay you? After all, you are the glue that holds the organization together. Remember that more than 4.2 million women work in this capacity, according to a 1994 Bureau of Labor Statistics report, making this group the largest category of working women in the United States. And that number is expected to grow by more than 250,000 by the year 2005. With these statistics, you can make a great impact on management and your organizations.

Support staff needs to be more proactive and to take a stronger stand for itself. Assistants need to ask their managers to schedule daily or weekly meetings, seek pay increases based on performance, ask for the bigger picture, ask for acknowledgment, and ask for clear career paths. It is time for support staff to stand up and be counted.

The purpose of this book was to inspire your learning and to improve your value to yourselves and to your organizations. The suggestions, tips, and exercises for productive ways to think (the Five Core Competencies) and for actions you can take (the Productivity Cycle) are geared to helping you produce valuable results and improve the quality of your work life. Figure 14-1 is the essence of this book; take it to heart.

Figure 14-1. Summary for Success.

R ecognize the valuable contribution you make to your organization. You are an integral part of your company's success. Acknowledge yourself and others for work well done.

E mpower yourself and others. Share what you have learned in this book with your manager and your coworkers. It takes a team, working productively together, to produce results that satisfy customers.

S earch for opportunities to invent and innovate in your job. Find new ways to contribute to customer satisfaction.

U tilize the Five Core Competencies and the Productivity Cycle™ to become a results producer.

L isten and speak effectively. Good communication is key to creating valuable results and satisfying customers.

T ake control of the quality of your work life! Create the job satisfaction you want. Go for it!

Index

accountability, 66–68
  announcing completed results, 156–157
  assessing, 56, 67–68, 71–73
  blaming others, 61–62
  case study, 62–64, 68–71
  communication, effective, 59, 108, 113–114, 116–117
  daily practice, 65
  decision making, 143
  defining, 48
  mistakes, acknowledging, 60–61
  requests in productivity cycle, 127, 134–135, 138–139, 151, 158, 160
acknowledging barriers, 85
acknowledging completed results, 160–162
actions creating results, 87, 95–96, 121–123, 154
active listening, 112
act stage in learning process, 101, 102
administration
  clueless managers, 33–36
  controlling managers, 36–39
  decrease in, 12
  leaders, true, 40–44
  middle managers, 12, 165

American Management Association (AMA), 10
announcing completed results, 156–157
anticipating and resolving barriers, 87, 155
assessment
  accountability, 56, 67–68, 71–73
  barriers, 87
  and belief that barriers are opportunities, 57
  communication, effective, 59, 116–117
  learning process, 58
  productivity, 50–59
  productivity cycle, 157–160
  results, commitment to, 57–58
  self-, 27–28
authority, lack of, 75
authority, misuse of, 79

band-aid approach, 77, 79
Barker, Joel, on paradigm shifts, 15, 19
barriers, 74
  see also belief that barriers are opportunities
behavioral responses, productive, 85–87
belief that barriers are opportunities
  assessing, 57

belief that barriers are opportunities (*continued*)
  behavior influenced by, 17
  conflicts, 78–83
  defining, 48
  problems, defining, 74–77
  productive stance, 85–87
  resolving a current breakdown,
    88
  unproductive stance, 84–85
best practices companies, 2
blaming others, 61–62, 65–66, 84
Bravo, Ellen, on trends in support
  staff, 1–2, 166
busy bee work style, 29–30, 31,
  34–35, 37–38, 42

case studies, 62–64, 68–71, 97
change, organizational, 7–14, 18–
  24, 76
chaos, 18
checklist for effective communication, 117–118
chronological progression of paradigm shifts, 19–22
clarifying requests in productivity cycle, 137–142
clarity about results, 91–92
clueless managers, 33–36
commitment to results, 94–95
  see also results, commitment to
communication, effective
  accountability, 108
  assessing, 59, 116–117
  checklist for, 117–118
  defining, 49
  language, 110–111
  listening skills, 111–116
  requests, making, 135–137
  results, commitment to, 123
  timing, 109–110
  tone, 111
  training needed, 8

companies
  best-practices, 2
  change, organizational, 7–14,
    18–24, 76
  conforming to expectations of,
    18
  downsizing/restructuring de-
    mands, 11, 12, 23, 49
  job descriptions, 49–50
  paradigm shifts, 17–18
  profits, 8, 9, 121
  progressive, 9
  value of employees, recogniz-
    ing, 1, 8
competencies, five core, 47
  accountability, 60–73
  assessing your productivity,
    50–59
  belief that barriers are opportu-
    nities, 74–89
  communication, effective,
    108–118
  defining, 48–49
  failure to practice, 75, 76
  learning process, 99–108
  results, commitment to, 90–98
computer technology, 8, 11
confidence to get work needs met,
  3, 7, 9–13, 16, 24, 166
conflicts, 78–83
conforming to company expectations, 18
controlling managers, 36–39
culture, company, 18
customers, 8, 11, 121, 139, 155

daily practice, putting accountability into, 65
decision making, 143–150
desire to learn, 99–108
desk potato work style, 29, 31, 33–
  34, 36–37, 41

Discovering the Future (Barker), 15
downsizing, 11, 23, 49

emotions, 82
explore stage in learning process,
    101

feedback, 27–28
focusing on results, not tasks,
    90–91
future business trends, 11

gender and support staff, 2
Germany, training in, 8

health care costs, 27
Hewlett-Packard, 9
hiding, 84
hot-button words, 110

ignoring, 84
"I" messages, 81, 82
implementing plans, 87, 95–96,
    121–123, 154
improvement, continuous, 100
incompetence, acknowledging,
    104
information, lack of, 75, 79
information age, 11
Intel, 9
interpersonal skills, 12

Japan, training in, 8
job descriptions, 49–50
job titles, 10

knowledge, defining, 9
Kuhn, Thomas, on belief systems,
    17

labeling employees, 18
language, 110–111

leaders, true, 40–44
learning process, 99
    assessing, 58
    defining, 49
    guidelines, 107
    meddler vs. player voice, 103
    skills, new, 105–106
    stages in, 101–102
    success, keys to, 104
    why learn, 100
listening skills, 82, 111–116, 136
long-term solutions, 78
look stage in learning process, 101

manager-assistant relationship, 3
    being taken for granted, 2
    busy bees and clueless manag-
        ers, 34–35
    busy bees and controlling man-
        agers, 37–38
    busy bees and true leaders, 42
    desk potatoes and clueless
        managers, 33–34
    desk potatoes and controlling
        managers, 36–37
    desk potatoes and true leaders,
        41
    key elements, 13
    restructuring demands, 12
    results producers and clueless
        managers, 35–36
    results producers and control-
        ling managers, 39
    results producers and true
        leaders, 42–43
    work styles, 27
martyrdom, 65
meddler voice, 103–104
mentors, 104
middle management, 12, 165
mistakes, human, 60–61, 66, 75–
    76, 82

monitoring progress, 96
moods, counterproductive, 75, 79
myths about barriers, 82–83

negative events, taking responsi-
    bility for, 62
negotiating, 149
neutral terms, 82
1960s and paradigm shifts, 22–23
no, saying, 145–149
nonessential support staff, 2
Northern Telecom, 9
notice stage in learning process,
    101, 102

office scene, the changing, 7–14,
    18–24

panicking, 84
paradigm shifts, 15–24, 165
paralyzed, becoming, 85
parental messages and traditional
    assistants, 22
perceptions, principles of
    changing
  organizational change, 7–14
  paradigm shifts, 15–24
  problem or breakdown, 78
  productivity, 25–44
Peters, Tom, on chaos, 18
Peters, Tom, on training employ-
    ees, 8
planning for results, 96, 151–154
player voice, 103, 104
policies/procedures, change in,
    76
positive events, taking responsi-
    bility for, 62
positive intentions and conflict
    resolution, 81
preparing requests, 127–134

proactive stance, taking a, 3, 7,
    9–13, 16, 24, 166
problems, 74–77
    see also belief that barriers are
      opportunities
productivity, 25–26
  assessing, 50–59
  barriers, responses to, 83, 85–87
  clueless managers, 33–36
  controlling managers, 36–39
  defining, 13
  profiles of work styles, 28–32
  stress decreased with in-
      creased, 13–14
  and true leaders, 40–44
  work styles and, link between,
      26–28
productivity cycle, 121–123
  acknowledging completed re-
      sults, 160–162
  announcing completed results,
      156–157
  assessing results, 157–160
  clarifying requests, 137–142
  decision making, 143–150
  making requests, 134–137
  personal perspective, 126
  preparing the requests, 127–134
  results, producing, 150–155
  team perspective, 123–125
Professional Secretaries Interna-
    tional (PSI), 2, 8
profits, 8, 9, 121

questions, asking, 104

reflecting, 87
repeat and practice stage in learn-
    ing process, 101, 102
requesting and commitment to re-
    sults, 96

requests in productivity cycle
  accountability, 151, 158, 160
  clarifying, 137–142
  making, 134–137
  preparing, 127–134
resources needed to create results, 93
respect for support staff, 2, 23
responsibilities of support staff, 2, 24, 49–50
restructuring demands, 11, 12, 23, 49
results, commitment to, 94–95
  actions, 87, 95–96, 121–123, 154
  assessing, 57–58
  being clear about intended results, 91–92
  defining, 49
  focusing on results not tasks, 90–91
  guidelines, 97–98
  productivity cycle, 139–140, 150–162
  resources, securing, 93
results producer work style, 30, 31–32, 35–36, 39, 42–43
risk taking, 7, 24, 64, 165

salary for support staff, 2
Seagram Wine Classics, 9
self-assessment, 27–28
skills, lack of specific, 75–77
skills, learning new, 100–101, 105–106
societal messages and traditional assistants, 22, 23
software and database programs, 8, 11
solutions, best, 77–78
specific skills, lack of, 75–77
stereotypical roles, 22–23

stress, 13–14
Structure of Scientific Revolutions, The (Kuhn), 17
success, summary for, 167

team building, 8, 12, 123–125
technical skills, 12
technological innovation, 10, 113
Thriving on Chaos (Peters), 8, 18
time, lack of, 75, 76
time and profits, 9
timing in communication, 109–110
tone in communication, 111
traditional assistant, 16–17, 22
training, 8–12, 49
trends affecting support staff in 1990s, 1–2

unaccountable stance, 63
unexpected situations, 75, 76
unproductive responses to barriers, 83–85

value of support staff, 1, 8
Varian Associates, 9
victim, thinking of yourself as a, 61

workspace, shared, 79–81
work styles
  busy bee, 34–35, 37–38, 42
  desk potato, 33–34, 36–37, 41
  merging gaps in, 3
  proactive stance, taking a, 17
  productivity and, links between, 26–28
  profiling, 28–32
  results producer, 35–36, 39, 42–43

yes, saying, 145

If you would like any additional information about the services offered by Executive Counterparts, please call (415) 616-9901 or write to 760 Market Street, Suite 745, San Francisco, CA 94102.

The web-site is www.ExecutiveCounterparts.com
The e-mail is michelle@executivecounterparts.com